BORDERS®
CLASSICS

FOUR CENTURIES OF GREAT LOVE POEMS

Compiled by Debra Starr

BORDERS.
CLASSICS

Please direct sales or editorial inquiries to:
BordersTradeBookInventoryQuestions@bordersgroupinc.com

This edition is published by
Borders Classics, an imprint of Borders Group, Inc.,
by special arrangement with
Ann Arbor Media Group, LLC
2500 South State Street, Ann Arbor, MI 48104

Printed and bound in the United States of America
by Edwards Brothers, Inc.

Quality Paperback ISBN13: 978-1-58726-455-9
ISBN10: 1-58726-455-2

10   09   08   07   06   10 9 8 7 6 5 4 3 2

CONTENTS

THE DEFINITION OF LOVE

COME LIVE WITH ME
AND BE MY LOVE

It Was a Lover and His Lass

William Shakespeare

It was a lover and his lass,
　　With a hey, and a ho, and a hey nonino,
That o'er the green cornfield did pass,
　　In springtime, the only pretty ring time,
When birds do sing, hey ding a ding, ding;
Sweet lovers love the spring.

Between the acres of the rye,
　　With a hey, and a ho, and a hey nonino,
Those pretty country folks would lie,
　　In springtime, the only pretty ring time,
When birds do sing, hey ding a ding, ding;
Sweet lovers love the spring.

This carol they began that hour,
　　With a hey, and a ho, and a hey nonino,
How that a life was but a flower
　　In springtime, the only pretty ring time,
When birds do sing, hey ding a ding, ding;
Sweet lovers love the spring.

And therefore take the present time,
　　With a hey, and a ho, and a hey nonino,
For love is crownèd with the prime
　　In springtime, the only pretty ring time,
When birds do sing, hey ding a ding, ding;
Sweet lovers love the spring.

The Passionate Shepherd to His Love

CHRISTOPHER MARLOWE

Come live with me and be my love,
And we will all the pleasures prove,
That hills and valleys, dales and fields,
And all the craggy mountains yields.

There we will sit upon the rocks,
And see the shepherds feed their flocks,
By shallow rivers to whose falls
Melodious birds sing madrigals.

And I will make thee beds of roses
With a thousand fragrant posies,
A cap of flowers, and a kirtle
Embroidered all with leaves of myrtle;

A gown made of the finest wool
Which from our pretty lambs we pull;
Fair lined slippers for the cold,
With buckles of the purest gold;

A belt of straw and ivy buds,
With coral clasps and amber studs:
And if these pleasures may thee move,
Come live with me and be my love.

The shepherds' swains shall dance and sing
For thy delight each May morning:
If these delights thy mind may move,
Then live with me and be my love.

The Nymph's Reply to the Shepherd

SIR WALTER RALEIGH

If all the world and love were young,
And truth in every shepherd's tongue,
These pretty pleasures might me move,
To live with thee, and be thy love.

Time drives the flocks from field to fold,
When rivers rage, and rocks grow cold,
And Philomel becometh dumb,
The rest complains of cares to come.

The flowers do fade, and wanton fields,
To wayward winter reckoning yields,
A honey tongue, a heart of gall,
Is fancy's spring, but sorrow's fall.

Thy gowns, thy shoes, thy beds of roses,
Thy cap, thy kirtle, and thy posies,
Soon break, soon wither, soon forgotten:
In folly ripe, in reason rotten.

Thy belt of straw and ivy buds,
Thy coral clasps and amber studs,
All these in me no means can move,
To come to thee, and be thy love.

But could youth last, and love still breed,
Had joys no date, nor age no need,
Then these delights my mind might move,
To live with thee and be thy love.

To Jane: The Invitation

Percy Bysshe Shelley

Best and brightest, come away!
Fairer far than this fair Day,
Which, like thee to those in sorrow,
Comes to bid a sweet good-morrow
To the rough Year just awake
In its cradle on the brake.
The brightest hour of unborn Spring,
Through the winter wandering,
Found, it seems, the halcyon Morn
To hoar February born.
Bending from Heaven, in azure mirth,
It kissed the forehead of the Earth,
And smiled upon the silent sea,
And bade the frozen streams be free,
And waked to music all their fountains,
And breathed upon the frozen mountains,
And like a prophetess of May
Strewed flowers upon the barren way,
Making the wintry world appear
Like one on whom thou smilest, dear.
Away, away, from men and towns,
To the wild wood and the downs—
To the silent wilderness
Where the soul need not repress
Its music lest it should not find
An echo in another's mind.
While the touch of Nature's art
Harmonizes heart to heart.
I leave this notice on my door
For each accustomed visitor:—
"I am gone into the fields
To take what this sweet hour yields;—
Reflection, you may come tomorrow,

Sit by the fireside with Sorrow.—
You with the unpaid bill, Despair,—
You, tiresome verse-reciter, Care,—
I will pay you in the grave,—
Death will listen to your stave.
Expectation too, be off!
Today is for itself enough;
Hope, in pity mock not Woe
With smiles, nor follow where I go;
Long having lived on thy sweet food,
At length I find one moment's good
After long pain—with all your love,
This you never told me of."

Radiant Sister of the Day,
Awake! arise! and come away!
To the wild woods and the plains,
And the pools where winter rains
Image all their roof of leaves,
Where the pine its garland weaves
Of sapless green and ivy dun
Round stems that never kiss the sun:
Where the lawns and pastures be,
And the sandhills of the sea:—
Where the melting hoar-frost wets
The daisy-star that never sets,
And wind-flowers, and violets,
Which yet join not scent to hue,
Crown the pale year weak and new;
When the night is left behind
In the deep east, dun and blind,
And the blue noon is over us,
And the multitudinous
Billows murmur at our feet,
Where the earth and ocean meet,
And all things seem only one
In the universal sun.

Go, Lovely Rose

Edmund Waller

Go, lovely Rose—
　Tell her that wastes her time and me,
　That now she knows,
When I resemble her to thee,
How sweet and fair she seems to be.

　Tell her that's young,
And shuns to have her graces spied,
　That hadst thou sprung
In deserts where no men abide,
Thou must have uncommended died.

　Small is the worth
Of beauty from the light retired:
　Bid her come forth,
Suffer herself to be desired,
And not blush so to be admired.

　Then die—that she
The common fate of all things rare
　May read in thee;
How small a part of time they share
That are so wondrous sweet and fair!

Song to Celia

BEN JONSON

Come my Celia, let us prove,
While we may, the sports of love.
Time will not be ours for ever:
He at length our good will sever.
Spend not then his gifts in vain;
Suns that set may rise again,
But if once we lose this light
'Tis, with us, perpetual night.
Why should we defer our joys?
Fame and rumour are but toys.
Cannot we delude the eyes
Of a few poor household spies?
Or his easier ears beguile,
So removed by our wile?
'Tis no sin love's fruit to steal,
But the sweet theft to reveal;
To be taken, to be seen,
These have crimes accounted been.

Stanzas

MARY WOLLSTONECRAFT SHELLEY

Oh, come to me in dreams, my love!
  I will not ask a dearer bliss;
Come with the starry beams, my love,
  And press mine eyelids with thy kiss.

'Twas thus, as ancient fables tell,
  Love visited a Grecian maid,
Till she disturbed the sacred spell,
  And woke to find her hopes betrayed.

But gentle sleep shall veil my sight,
  And Psyche's lamp shall darkling be,
When, in the visions of the night,
  Thou dost renew thy vows to me.

Then come to me in dreams, my love,
  I will not ask a dearer bliss;
Come with the starry beams, my love,
  And press mine eyelids with thy kiss.

To the Virgins, To Make Much of Time

ROBERT HERRICK

Gather ye rosebuds while ye may,
  Old Time is still a-flying:
And this same flower that smiles today
  Tomorrow will be dying.

The glorious lamp of heaven, the sun,
  The higher he's a-getting,
The sooner will his race be run.
  And nearer he's to setting.

That age is best which is the first,
  When youth and blood are warmer;
But being spent, the worse, and worst
  Times still succeed the former.

Then be not coy, but use your time,
  And while ye may, go marry:
For having lost but once your prime,
  You may for ever tarry.

Sonnet from the Portuguese XXXV

Elizabeth Barrett Browning

If I leave all for thee, wilt thou exchange
And be all to me? Shall I never miss
Home-talk and blessing and the common kiss
That comes to each in turn, nor count it strange,
When I look up, to drop on a new range
Of walls and floors, . . . another home than this?
Nay, wilt thou fill that place by me which is
Filled by dead eyes too tender to know change?
That's hardest. If to conquer love, has tried,
To conquer grief, tries more, as all things prove,
For grief indeed is love and grief beside.
Alas, I have grieved so I am hard to love.
Yet love me—wilt thou? Open thine heart wide,
And fold within, the wet wings of thy dove.

To His Coy Mistress

ANDREW MARVELL

Had we but world enough, and time,
This coyness, Lady, were no crime.
We would sit down and think which way
To walk and pass our long love's day.
Thou by the Indian Ganges' side
Shouldst rubies find: I by the tide
Of Humber would complain. I would
Love you ten years before the Flood,
And you should, if you please, refuse
Till the conversion of the Jews.
My vegetable love should grow
Vaster than empires, and more slow;
An hundred years should go to praise
Thine eyes and on thy forehead gaze;
Two hundred to adore each breast;
But thirty thousand to the rest:
An age at least to every part,
And the last age should show your heart;
For, Lady, you deserve this state,
Nor would I love at lower rate.
    But at my back I always hear
Time's wingèd chariot hurrying near:
And yonder all before us lie
Deserts of vast eternity.
Thy beauty shall no more be found,
Nor, in thy marble vault, shall sound
My echoing song: then worms shall try
That long preserved virginity,
And your quaint honour turn to dust,
And into ashes all my lust:
The grave's a fine and private place,
But none, I think, do there embrace.

Now therefore, while the youthful hue
Sits on thy skin like morning dew,
And while thy willing soul transpires
At every pore with instant fires,
Now let us sport us while we may,
And now, like amorous birds of prey,
Rather at once our time devour
Than languish in his slow-chapt power.
Let us roll all our strength and all
Our sweetness up into one ball,
And tear our pleasures with rough strife
Thorough the iron gates of life:
Thus, though we cannot make our sun
Stand still, yet we will make him run.

The Flight

Sara Teasdale

Look back with longing eyes and know that I will follow,
Lift me up in your love as a light wing lifts a swallow,
Let our flight be far in sun or blowing rain—
But what if I heard my first love calling me again?

Hold me on your heart as the brave sea holds the foam,
Take me far away to the hills that hide your home:
Peace shall thatch the roof and love shall latch the door—
But what if I heard my first love calling me once more?

Look, Delia, How We Esteem the Half-Blown Rose

SAMUEL DANIEL

Look, Delia, how we esteem the half-blown rose,
The image of thy blush, and summer's honour!
Whilst yet her tender bud doth undisclose
That full of beauty Time bestows upon her.
No sooner spreads her glory in the air
But straight her wide-blown pomp comes to decline;
She then is scorned that late adorned the fair;

So fade the roses of those cheeks of thine.
No April can revive thy withered flowers,
Whose springing grace adorns thy glory now;
Swift, speedy Time, feathered with flying hours,
Dissolves the beauty of the fairest brow.
Then do not thou such treasure waste in vain,
But love now, whilst thou mayst be loved again.

Love's Philosophy

PERCY BYSSHE SHELLEY

The fountains mingle with the river
　And the rivers with the ocean,
The winds of heaven mix for ever
　With a sweet emotion;
Nothing in the world is single;
　All things by a law divine
In one spirit meet and mingle.
　Why not I with thine?—

See the mountains kiss high heaven
　And the waves clasp one another;
No sister-flower would be forgiven
　If it disdained its brother;
And the sunlight clasps the earth
　And the moonbeams kiss the sea:
What is all this sweet work worth
　If thou kiss not me?

SHALL I COMPARE THEE TO A SUMMER'S DAY?

Shall I Compare Thee to a Summer's Day?

WILLIAM SHAKESPEARE

Shall I compare thee to a summer's day?
Thou art more lovely and more temperate:
Rough winds do shake the darling buds of May,
And summer's lease hath all too short a date:
Sometime too hot the eye of heaven shines,
And often is his gold complexion dimmed;
And every fair from fair sometime declines,
By chance, or nature's changing course untrimmed;
But thy eternal summer shall not fade,
Nor lose possession of that fair thou owest,
Nor shall Death brag thou wander'st in his shade,
When in eternal lines to time thou growest;
   So long as men can breathe, or eyes can see,
   So long lives this, and this gives life to thee.

Song

ROBERT BROWNING

Nay but you, who do not love her,
  Is she not pure gold, my mistress?
Holds earth aught—speak truth—above her?
  Aught like this tress, see, and this tress,
And this last fairest tress of all,
So fair, see, ere I let it fall?

Because you spend your lives in praising;
  To praise, you search the wide world over:
Then why not witness, calmly gazing,
  If earth holds aught—speak truth—above her?
Above this tress, and this, I touch
But cannot praise, I love so much!

First Love

John Clare

I ne'er was struck before that hour
  With love so sudden and so sweet,
Her face it bloomed like a sweet flower
  And stole my heart away complete.

My face turned pale as deadly pale,
  My legs refused to walk away,
And when she looked, what could I ail?
  My life and all seemed turned to clay.

And then my blood rushed to my face
  And took my eyesight quite away,
The trees and bushes round the place
  Seemed midnight at noonday.

I could not see a single thing,
  Words from my eyes did start—
They spoke as chords do from the string,
  And blood burnt round my heart.

Are flowers the winter's choice?
  Is love's bed always snow?
She seemed to hear my silent voice,
I never saw so sweet a face
  As that I stood before.
My heart has left its dwelling-place
  And can return no more.

She Was a Phantom of Delight

WILLIAM WORDSWORTH

She was a phantom of delight
When first she gleamed upon my sight;
A lovely apparition, sent
To be a moment's ornament;
Her eyes as stars of twilight fair;
Like twilight's too, her dusky hair;
But all things else about her drawn
From May-time and the cheerful dawn;
A dancing shape, an image gay,
To haunt, to startle, and waylay.

I saw her upon nearer view,
A spirit, yet a woman too!
Her household motions light and free,
And steps of virgin-liberty;
A countenance in which did meet
Sweet records, promises as sweet;
A creature not too bright or good
For human nature's daily food;
For transient sorrows, simple wiles,
Praise, blame, love, kisses, tears, and smiles.

And now I see with eye serene
The very pulse of the machine;
A being breathing thoughtful breath,
A traveller between life and death;
The reason firm, the temperate will,
Endurance, foresight, strength, and skill;
A perfect woman, nobly planned,
To warn, to comfort, and command;
And yet a spirit still, and bright
With something of angelic light.

A Birthday

Christina Rossetti

My heart is like a singing bird
Whose nest is in a watered shoot;
My heart is like an apple tree
Whose boughs are bent with thickset fruit;
My heart is like a rainbow shell
That paddles in a halcyon sea;
My heart is gladder than all these
Because my love is come to me.

Raise me a dais of silk and down;
Hang it with vair and purple dyes;
Carve it in doves and pomegranates,
And peacocks with a hundred eyes;
Work it in gold and silver grapes,
In leaves and silver fleurs-de-lys;
Because the birthday of my life
Is come, my love is come to me.

My Life's Delight

Thomas Campion

Come, O come, my life's delight,
  Let me not in languor pine!
Love loves no delay; thy sight,
  The more enjoyed, the more divine:
O come, and take from me
The pain of being deprived of thee!

Thou all sweetness dost enclose,
  Like a little world of bliss.
Beauty guards thy looks: the rose
  In them pure and eternal is.
Come, then, and make thy flight
As swift to me, as heavenly light.

Who Is Silvia?

WILLIAM SHAKESPEARE

Who is Silvia? what is she,
    That all our swains commend her?
Holy, fair, and wise is she;
    The heaven such grace did lend her,
That she might admirèd be.

Is she kind as she is fair?
    For beauty lives with kindness.
Love doth to her eyes repair,
    To help him of his blindness;
And, being helped, inhabits there.

Then to Silvia let us sing,
    That Silvia is excelling;
She excels each mortal thing
    Upon the dull earth dwelling;
To her let us garlands bring

Upon Julia's Clothes

ROBERT HERRICK

Whenas in silks my Julia goes
Then, then (methinks) how sweetly flows
That liquefaction of her clothes.

Next, when I cast mine eyes and see
That brave vibration each way free;
O how that glittering taketh me!

The Constant Lover

SIR JOHN SUCKLING

Out upon it, I have loved
   Three whole days together!
And am like to love three more,
   If it prove fair weather.

Time shall moult away his wings
   Ere he shall discover
In the whole wide world again
   Such a constant lover.

But the spite on 't is, no praise
   Is due at all to me:
Love with me had made no stays,
   Had it any been but she.

Had it any been but she,
   And that very face,
There had been at least ere this
   A dozen dozen in her place.

To —

JOHN KEATS

Had I a man's fair form, then might my sighs
  Be echoed swiftly through that ivory shell
  Thine ear, and find thy gentle heart; so well
  Would passion arm me for the enterprise:
But ah! I am no knight whose foeman dies;
  No cuirass glistens on my bosom's swell;
  I am no happy shepherd of the dell
  Whose lips have trembled with a maiden's eyes.
Yet must I dote upon thee—call thee sweet,
  Sweeter by far than Hybla's honied roses
  When steep'd in dew rich to intoxication.
Ah! I will taste that dew, for me 'tis meet,
  And when the moon her pallid face discloses,
  I'll gather some by spells, and incantation.

Madrigal

William Drummond

Like the Idalian queen,
Her hair about her eyne,
With neck and breast's ripe apples to be seen,
At first glance of the morn
In Cyprus' gardens gathering those fair flowers
Which of her blood were born,
I saw, but fainting saw, my paramours.
The Graces naked danced about the place,
The winds and trees amazed
With silence on her gazed,
The flowers did smile, like those upon her face;
And as their aspen stalks those fingers band,
That she might read my case,
A hyacinth I wished me in her hand.

To Helen

Edgar Allan Poe

Helen, thy beauty is to me
  Like those Nicean barks of yore.
That gently, o'er a perfumed sea,
  The weary, wayworn wanderer bore
  To his own native shore.

On desperate seas long wont to roam,
  Thy hyacinth hair, thy classic face,
Thy Naiad airs have brought me home
  To the glory that was Greece,
  To the grandeur that was Rome.

Lo! in yon brilliant window niche,
  How statue-like I see thee stand,
  The agate lamp within thy hand!
Ah, Psyche, from the regions which
  Are Holy Land!

My Mistress' Eyes Are Nothing Like the Sun

WILLIAM SHAKESPEARE

My mistress' eyes are nothing like the sun;
Coral is far more red than her lips' red:
If snow be white, why then her breasts are dun;
If hairs be wires, black wires grow on her head.
I have seen roses damaskt, red and white,
But no such roses see I in her cheeks;
And in some perfumes is there more delight
Than in the breath that from my mistress reeks.
I love to hear her speak, yet well I know
That music hath a far more pleasing sound;
I grant I never saw a goddess go;
My mistress, when she walks, treads on the ground.
   And yet, by heaven, I think my love as rare
   As any she belied with false compare.

Drink to Me Only with Thine Eyes

BEN JONSON

Drink to me only with thine eyes,
　And I will pledge with mine;
Or leave a kiss but in the cup
　And I'll not look for wine.
The thirst that from the soul doth rise
　Doth ask a drink divine;
But might I of Jove's nectar sup,
　I would not change for thine.

I sent thee late a rosy wreath,
　Not so much honoring thee
As giving it a hope that there
　It could not withered be;
But thou thereon didst only breathe,
　And sent'st it back to me;
Since when it grows, and smells, I swear,
　Not of itself, but thee!

How Many Paltry, Foolish, Painted Things

Michael Drayton

How many paltry, foolish, painted things,
That now in coaches trouble every street,
Shall be forgotten, whom no poet sings,
Ere they be well wrapt in their winding-sheet!
Where I to thee eternity shall give,
When nothing else remaineth of these days,
And queens hereafter shall be glad to live
Upon the alms of thy superfluous praise.
Virgins and matrons, reading these my rimes,
Shall be so much delighted with thy story
That they shall grieve they lived not in these times,
To have seen thee, their sex's only glory.
So shalt thou fly above the vulgar throng,
Still to survive in my immortal song.

To Anthea, Who May Command Him Anything

ROBERT HERRICK

Bid me to live, and I will live
    Thy protestant to be:
Or bid me love, and I will give
    A loving heart to thee.

A heart as soft, a heart as kind,
    A heart as sound and free
As in the whole world thou canst find,
    That heart I'll give to thee.

Bid that heart stay, and it will stay,
    To honor thy decree:
Or bid it languish quite away,
    And 't shall do so for thee.

Bid me to weep, and I will weep
    While I have eyes to see:
And having none, yet I will keep
    A heart to weep for thee.

Bid me despair, and I'll despair,
    Under that cypress tree:
Or bid me die, and I will dare
    E'en Death, to die for thee.

Thou art my life, my love, my heart,
    The very eyes of me,
And hast command of every part,
    To live and die for thee.

Night of Love

PAUL LAURENCE DUNBAR

The moon has left the sky, love,
The stars are hiding now,
And frowning on the world, love,
Night bares her sable brow.

The snow is on the ground, love,
And cold and keen the air is.
I'm singing here to you, love;
You're dreaming there in Paris.

But this is Nature's law, love,
Though just it may not seem,
That men should wake to sing, love;
While maidens sleep and dream.

Them care may not molest, love,
Nor stir them from their slumbers,
Though midnight find the swain, love.
Still halting o'er his numbers.

I watch the rosy dawn, love,
Come stealing up the east,
While all things round rejoice, love,
That Night her reign has ceased.

The lark will soon be heard, love,
And on his way be winging;
When Nature's poets wake, love,
Why should a man be singing?

She Walks in Beauty

George Gordon, Lord Byron

She walks in beauty, like the night
　Of cloudless climes and starry skies;
And all that's best of dark and bright
　Meet in her aspect and her eyes:
Thus mellowed to that tender light
　Which heaven to gaudy day denies.

One shade the more, one ray the less,
　Had half impaired the nameless grace
Which waves in every raven tress,
　Or softly lightens o'er her face;
Where thoughts serenely sweet express
　How pure, how dear their dwelling place.

And on that cheek, and o'er that brow,
　So soft, so calm, yet eloquent,
The smiles that win, the tints that glow,
　But tell of days in goodness spent,
A mind at peace with all below,
　A heart whose love is innocent!

When in Disgrace

WILLIAM SHAKESPEARE

When in disgrace with fortune and men's eyes,
I all alone beweep my outcast state,
And trouble deaf heaven with my bootless cries,
And look upon myself, and curse my fate,
Wishing me like to one more rich in hope,
Featur'd like him, like him with friends possess'd,
Desiring this man's art, and that man's scope,
With what I most enjoy contented least;
Yet in these thoughts myself almost despising,
Haply I think on thee, and then my state,
Like to the lark at break of day arising
From sullen earth, sings hymns at heaven's gate;
   For thy sweet love rememb'red such wealth brings,
   That then I scorn to change my state with kings.

Let Others Sing of Knights

SAMUEL DANIEL

Let others sing of knights and paladins
In agèd accents and untimely words;
Paint shadows in imaginary lines,
Which well the reach of their high wits records:
But I must sing of thee, and those fair eyes
Authentic shall my verse in time to come;
When yet th' unborn shall say, "Lo where she lies,
Whose beauty made him speak that else was dumb."
These are the arks, the trophies I erect
That fortify thy name against old age;
And these thy sacred virtues must protect
Against the dark, and Time's consuming rage.
Though th' error of my youth in them appear,
Suffice they shew I lived and loved thee dear.

NO PLATONIC LOVE

Corinna's Going A-Maying

ROBERT HERRICK

Get up, get up for shame! The blooming morn
Upon her wings presents the god unshorn.
   See how Aurora throws her fair,
   Fresh-quilted colors through the air.
   Get up, sweet slug-a-bed, and see
   The dew bespangling herb and tree!
Each flower has wept and bowed toward the east
Above an hour since, yet you not drest;
   Nay! not so much as out of bed?
   When all the birds have matins said
   And sung their thankful hymns, 'tis sin,
   Nay, profanation, to keep in,
Whenas a thousand virgins on this day
Spring sooner than the lark, to fetch in May.

Rise and put on your foliage, and be seen
To come forth, like the springtime, fresh and green.
   And sweet as Flora. Take no care
   For jewels for your gown or hair.
   Fear not; the leaves will strew
   Gems in abundance upon you.
Besides, the childhood of the day has kept
Against you come, some orient pearls unwept.
   Come, and receive them while the light
   Hangs on the dew-locks of the night;
   And Titan on the eastern hill
   Retires himself, or else stands still
Till you come forth! Wash, dress, be brief in praying;
Few beads are best when once we go a-Maying.

Come, my Corinna, come; and coming, mark
How each field turns a street, each street a park,
   Made green and trimmed with trees! see how
   Devotion gives each house a bough

Or branch! each porch, each door, ere this,
    An ark, a tabernacle is,
Made up of white-thorn neatly interwove,
As if here were those cooler shades of love.
    Can such delights be in the street
    And open fields, and we not see't?
    Come, we'll abroad; and let's obey
    The proclamation made for May,
And sin no more, as we have done, by staying;
But, my Corinna, come, let's go a-Maying.

There's not a budding boy or girl this day
But is got up and gone to bring in May.
    A deal of youth ere this is come
    Back, and with white-thorn laden home.
    Some have dispatched their cakes and cream,
    Before that we have left to dream;
And some have wept and wooed, and plighted troth
And chose their priest, ere we can cast off sloth.
    Many a green-gown has been given,
    Many a kiss, both odd and even;
    Many a glance, too, has been sent
    From out the eye, love's firmament;
Many a jest told of the keys betraying
This night, and locks picked; yet we're not a-Maying!

Come, let us go, while we are in our prime,
And take the harmless folly of the time!
    We shall grow old apace, and die
    Before we know our liberty.
    Our life is short, and our days run
    As fast away as does the sun.
And, as a vapor or a drop of rain,
Once lost, can ne'er be found again,
    So when or you or I are made
    A fable, song, or fleeting shade,
    All love, all liking, all delight
    Lies drowned with us in endless night.
Then, while time serves, and we are but decaying,
Come, my Corinna, come, let's go a-Maying.

No Platonic Love

William Cartwright

Tell me no more of minds embracing minds,
  And hearts exchang'd for hearts;
That spirits spirits meet, as winds do winds,
  And mix their subt'lest parts;
That two unbodied essences may kiss,
And then like Angels, twist and feel one Bliss.

I was that silly thing that once was wrought
  To practise this thin love;
I climb'd from sex to soul, from soul to thought;
  But thinking there to move,
Headlong I rolled from thought to soul, and then
From soul I lighted at the sex again.

As some strict down-looked men pretend to fast,
  Who yet in closets eat;
So lovers who profess they spirits taste,
  Feed yet on grosser meat;
I know they boast they souls to souls convey,
Howe'r they meet, the body is the way.

Come, I will undeceive thee, they that tread
  Those vain aerial ways,
Are like young heirs and alchemists misled
  To waste their wealth and days,
For searching thus to be for ever rich,
They only find a med'cine for the itch.

The Miller's Daughter

Alfred, Lord Tennyson

It is the miller's daughter,
  And she is grown so dear, so dear,
That I would be the jewel
  That trembles at her ear:
For hid in ringlets day and night,
I'd touch her neck so warm and white.

And I would be the girdle
  About her dainty, dainty waist,
And her heart would beat against me,
  In sorrow and in rest:
And I should know if it beat right,
I'd clasp it round so close and tight.

And I would be the necklace,
  And all day long to fall and rise
Upon her balmy bosom,
  With her laughter or her sighs:
And I would lie so light, so light,
I scarce should be unclasped at night.

Delight in Disorder

Robert Herrick

A sweet disorder in the dress
Kindles in clothes a wantonness:
A lawn about the shoulders thrown
Into a fine distraction,
An erring lace, which here and there
Enthralls the crimson stomacher,
A cuff neglectful, and thereby
Ribbands to flow confusedly,
A winning wave (deserving note)
In the tempestuous petticoat,
A careless shoe-string, in whose tie
I see a wild civility,
Do more bewitch me, than when art
Is too precise in every part.

Kissing My Kate

Robert Burns

O, merry hae I been teethin a heckle
An merry hae I been shapin a spoon!
O, merry hae I been cloutin a kettle,
An kissin my Katie when a' was done!
O, a' the lang day I ca' at my hammer,
An a' the lang day I whistle and sing!
O, a' the lang night I cuddle my kimmer,
An a' the lang night as happy's a king!
Bitter in dool, I lickit my winnins
O marrying Bess, to gie her a slave:
Blest be the hour she cool'd in her linens
And blythe be the bird that sings on her grave
Come to my arms, my Katie, my Katie,
An come to my arms, and kiss me again!
Drunken or sober, here's to thee, Katie,
An blest be the day I did it again!

Kisses Desired

WILLIAM DRUMMOND

Though I with strange desire
To kiss those rosy lips am set on fire,
Yet will I cease to crave
Sweet touches in such store,
As he who long before
From Lesbia them in thousands did receive.
Heart mine, but once me kiss,
And I by that sweet bliss
Even swear to cease you to importune more;
Poor one no number is;
Another word of me ye shall not hear
After one kiss, but still one kiss, my dear.

Jenny Kiss'd Me

LEIGH HUNT

Jenny kiss'd me when we met,
 Jumping from the chair she sat in;
Time, you thief, who love to get
 Sweets into your list, put that in!
Say I'm weary, say I'm sad,
 Say that health and wealth have miss'd me,
Say I'm growing old, but add,
 Jenny kiss'd me.

Come Slowly, Eden!

Emily Dickinson

Come slowly, Eden!
Lips unused to thee,
Bashful, sip thy jasmines,
As the fainting bee,

Reaching late his flower,
Round her chamber hums,
Counts his nectars—enters,
And is lost in balms!

Now

ROBERT BROWNING

Out of your whole life give but a moment!
All of your life that has gone before,
All to come after it,—so you ignore,
So you make perfect the present,—condense,
In a rapture of rage, for perfection's endowment,
Thought and feeling and soul and sense—
Merged in a moment which gives me at last
You around me for once, you beneath me, above me—
Me—sure that despite of time future, time past,—
This tick of our life-time's one moment you love me!
How long such suspension may linger? Ah, Sweet—
The moment eternal—just that and no more—
When ecstasy's utmost we clutch at the core
While cheeks burn, arms open, eyes shut and lips meet!

Sonnet from the Portuguese XXXVIII

Elizabeth Barrett Browning

First time he kissed me, he but only kissed
The fingers of this hand wherewith I write,
And ever since it grew more clean and white, . . .
Slow to world-greetings . . quick with its "Oh, list,"
When the angels speak. A ring of amethyst
I could not wear here plainer to my sight,
Than that first kiss. The second passed in height
The first, and sought the forehead, and half missed,
Half falling on the hair. O beyond meed!
That was the chrism of love, which love's own crown,
With sanctifying sweetness, did precede.
The third, upon my lips, was folded down
In perfect, purple state! since when, indeed,
I have been proud and said, "My Love, my own."

The Daisy Follows Soft the Sun

Emily Dickinson

The daisy follows soft the sun,
And when his golden walk is done,
   Sits shyly at his feet.
He, waking, finds the flower near.
"Wherefore, marauder, art thou here?
   "Because, sir, love is sweet!"

We are the flower, Thou the sun!
Forgive us, if as days decline,
   We nearer steal to Thee,—
Enamoured of the parting west,
The peace, the flight, the amethyst,
   Night's possibility!

Meeting at Night

ROBERT BROWNING

The grey sea and the long black land:
And the yellow half-moon large and low;
And the startled little waves that leap
In fiery ringlets from their sleep,
As I gain the cove with pushing prow,
And quench its speed in the slushy sand.

Then a mile of warm sea-scented beach;
Three fields to cross till a farm appears;
A tap at the pane, the quick sharp scratch
And blue spurt of a lighted match,
And a voice less loud, thro' its joys and fears,
Than the two hearts beating each to each!

To His Mistress Going to Bed

John Donne

Come, Madam, come, all rest my powers defy,
Until I labour, I in labour lie.
The foe oft-times having the foe in sight,
Is tir'd with standing though he never fight.
Off with that girdle, like heaven's Zone glistering,
But a far fairer world encompassing.
Unpin that spangled breastplate which you wear,
That th'eyes of busy fools may be stopped there.
Unlace yourself, for that harmonious chime,
Tells me from you, that now it is bed time.
Off with that happy busk, which I envy,
That still can be, and still can stand so nigh.
Your gown going off, such beauteous state reveals,
As when from flowery meads th'hill's shadow steals.
Off with that wiry Coronet and shew
The hairy Diadem which on you doth grow:
Now off with those shoes, and then safely tread
In this love's hallow'd temple, this soft bed.
In such white robes, heaven's Angels used to be
Received by men; Thou Angel bringst with thee
A heaven like Mahomet's Paradise: and though
Ill spirits walk in white, we easily know,
By this these Angels from an evil sprite,
Those set our hairs, but these our flesh upright.
    Licence my roving hands, and let them go,
Before, behind, between, above, below.
O my America! my new-found-land,
My kingdom, safeliest when with one man mann'd,
My Mine of precious stones, My Empire,
How blest am I in this discovering thee!
To enter in these bonds, is to be free;
Then where my hand is set, my seal shall be.

Full nakedness! All joys are due to thee,
As souls unbodied, bodies uncloth'd must be,
To taste whole joys. Gems which you women use
Are like Atlanta's balls, cast in men's views,
That when a fool's eye lighteth on a Gem,
His earthly soul may covet theirs, not them.
Like pictures, or like books' gay coverings made
For lay-men, are all women thus array'd;
Themselves are mystic books, which only we
(Whom their imputed grace will dignify)
Must see reveal'd. Then since that I may know;
As liberally, as to a Midwife, shew
Thy self: cast all, yea, this white linen hence,
There is no penance due to innocence.
  To teach thee, I am naked first; why then
What needst thou have more covering than a man.

Stolen Pleasure

WILLIAM DRUMMOND

My sweet did sweetly sleep,
And on her rosy face
Stood tears of pearl, which beauty's self did weep;
I, wond'ring at her grace,
Did all amaz'd remain,
When Love said, "Fool, can looks thy wishes crown?
Time past comes not again."
Then did I me bow down,
And kissing her fair breast, lips, cheeks, and eyes
Prov'd here on earth the joys of paradise.

The Sun Rising

John Donne

Busy old fool, unruly Sun,
    Why dost thou thus,
Through windows, and through curtains call on us?
Must to thy motions lovers' seasons run?
    Saucy pedantic wretch, go chide
    Late school-boys, and sour 'prentices,
    Go tell court-huntsmen that the King will ride,
    Call country ants to harvest offices;
Love, all alike, no season knows, nor clime,
Nor hours, days, months, which are the rags of time.

    Thy beams, so reverend, and strong
    Why shouldst thou think?
I could eclipse and cloud them with a wink,
But that I would not lose her sight so long:
    If her eyes have not blinded thine,
    Look, and tomorrow late, tell me,
    Whether both the Indias of spice and mine
    Be where thou left'st them, or lie here with me.
Ask for those kings whom thou saw'st yesterday,
And thou shalt hear, 'All here in one bed lay.'

    She is all States, and all Princes, I;
    Nothing else is.
Princes do but play us; compar'd to this,
All honour's mimic; all wealth alchemy.
    Thou Sun art half as happy as we,
    In that the world's contracted thus;
    Thine age asks ease, and since thy duties be
    To warm the world, that's done in warming us.
Shine here to us, and thou art every where;
This bed thy centre is, these walls, thy sphere.

MY LOVE IS LIKE TO ICE, AND I TO FIRE

Spring

Thomas Carew

Now that the winter's gone, the earth hath lost
Her snow-white robes; and now no more the frost
Candies the grass, or casts an icy cream
Upon the silver lake or crystal stream:
But the warm sun thaws the benumbed earth,
And makes it tender; gives a sacred birth
To the dead swallow; wakes in hollow tree
The drowsy cuckoo and the humble-bee.
Now do a choir of chirping minstrels bring,
In triumph to the world, the youthful spring:
The valleys, hills, and woods in rich array
Welcome the coming of the longed-for May.

Now all things smile: only my love doth lower,
Nor hath the scalding noon-day sun the power
To melt that marble ice, which still doth hold
Her heart congealed, and makes her pity cold.
The ox, which lately did for shelter fly
Into the stall, doth now securely lie
In open fields; and love no more is made
By the fire-side, but in the cooler shade
Amyntas now doth with his Chloris sleep
Under a sycamore, and all things keep
Time with the season: only she doth carry
June in her eyes, in her heart January.

Loving in Truth

SIR PHILIP SIDNEY

Loving in truth, and fain in verse my love to show,
That she, dear she, might take some pleasure of my pain:
Pleasure might cause her read, reading might make her know,
Knowledge might pity win, and pity grace obtain,
   I sought fit words to paint the blackest face of woe,
Studying inventions fine, her wits to entertain:
Oft turning others' leaves to see if thence would flow
Some fresh and fruitful showers upon my sun-burn'd brain.
   But words came halting forth, wanting Invention's stay,
Invention, Nature's child, fled step-dame Study's blows,
And others' feet still seem'd but strangers in my way.
Thus great with child to speak, and helpless in my throes,
   Biting my trewand pen, beating myself for spite,
   Fool, said my Muse to me, look in thy heart and write.

I Find No Peace, and All My War Is Done

SIR THOMAS WYATT

I find no peace, and all my war is done,
I fear, and hope. I burn, and freeze like ice.
I fly above the wind, yet can I not arise.
And naught I have, and all the world I season.
That loseth nor locketh holdeth me in prison,
And holdeth me not, yet can I 'scape nowise:
Nor letteth me live nor die at my devise,
And yet of death it giveth me occasion.
Without eyen I see, and without tongue I 'plain;
I desire to perish, and yet I ask health;
I love another, and thus I hate myself;
I feed me in sorrow, and laugh at all my pain.
 Likewise displeaseth me both death and life,
 And my delight is causer of this strife.

To Lysander

Aphra Behn

(On some verses he writ, and asking more for his heart than it was worth.)

Take back the heart you with such caution give,
  Take the fond valu'd trifle back:
I hate love merchants that a trade wou'd drive
  And meanly cunning bargains make.

I care not how the busy market goes
  And scorn to chaffer for a price:
Love does one staple rate on all impose,
  Nor leaves it to the trader's choice.

A heart requires a heart unfeign'd and true,
  Though subtly you advance the price;
And ask a rate that simple love ne'er knew
  And the free trade monopolize.

An humble slave the buyer must become,
  She must not bate a look or glance
You will have all or you'll have none;
  See how love's market you inhance.

It's not enough I gave you heart for heart,
  But I must add my lips and eyes;
I must no smile or friendly kiss impart;
  But you must dun me with advice . . .

Be just, my lovely swain, and do not take
  Freedoms you'll not to me allow:
O give Aminta so much freedom back
  That she may rove as well as you.

Let us then love upon the honest square
  Since interest neither have design'd,
For the sly gamester, who ne'er plays me fair
  Must trick for trick expect to find.

From *Amoretti*

EDMUND SPENSER

My Love is like to ice, and I to fire:
How comes it then that this her cold so great
Is not dissolved through my so hot desire,
But harder grows the more I her entreat?
Or how comes it that my exceeding heat
Is not allayed by her heart-frozen cold,
But that I burn much more in boiling sweat,
And feel my flames augmented manifold?
What more miraculous thing may be told,
That fire, which all things melts, should harden ice,
And ice, which is congeal'd with senseless cold,
Should kindle fire by wonderful device?
    Such is the power of love in gentle mind,
    That it can alter all the course of kind.

So oft as I her beauty do behold,
And therewith do her cruelty compare,
I marvel of what substance was the mould
The which her made at once so cruel-fair.
Not earth; for her high thoughts more heavenly are:
Not water; for her love doth burn like fire:
Not air; for she is not so light or rare:
Not fire; for she doth freeze with faint desire.

Then needs another element inquire
Whereof she might be made; that is, the sky.
For to the heaven her haughty looks aspire,
And eke her love is pure immortal high.
    Then since to heaven ye likened are the best,
    Be like in mercy as in all the rest.

Barbara Allen

ANONYMOUS

In Scarlet town, where I was born,
  There was a fair maid dwellin',
Made every youth cry *Well-a-way!*
  Her name was Barbara Allen.

All in the merry month of May,
  When green buds they were swellin',
Young Jemmy Grove on his death-bed lay,
  For love of Barbara Allen.

He sent his man in to her then,
  To the town where she was dwellin';
"O haste and come to my master dear,
  If your name be Barbara Allen."

So slowly, slowly rase she up,
  And slowly she came nigh him,
And when she drew the curtain by—
  "Young man, I think you're dyin'."

"O it's I am sick and very very sick,
  And it's all for Barbara Allen."—
"O the better for me ye'se never be,
  Tho' your heart's blood were a-spillin'!

"O dinna ye mind, young man," says she,
  "When the red wine ye were fillin',
That ye made the healths go round and round,
  And slighted Barbara Allen?"

He turned his face unto the wall,
  And death was with him dealin':
"Adieu, adieu, my dear friends all,
  And be kind to Barbara Allen!"

As she was walking o'er the fields,
　She heard the dead-bell knellin';
And every jow the dead-bell gave
　Cried "Woe to Barbara Allen."

"O mother, mother, make my bed,
　O make it saft and narrow:
My love has died for me today,
　I'll die for him tomorrow."

"Farewell," she said, "ye virgins all,
　And shun the fault I fell in:
Henceforth take warning by the fall
　Of cruel Barbara Allen."

A Complaint by Night

Henry Howard, Earl of Surrey

Alas! so all things now do hold their peace,
Heaven and earth disturbèd in no thing.
The beasts, the air, the birds their song do cease;
The nightès chare the stars about doth bring;
Calm is the sea; the waves work less and less.
So am not I, whom love, alas! doth wring,
Bringing before my face the great increase
Of my desires, whereat I weep and sing,
In joy and woe, as in a doubtful ease:
For my sweet thoughts sometime do pleasure bring;
But by and by, the cause of my disease
Gives me a pang, that inwardly doth sting,
When that I think what grief it is again,
To live and lack the thing should rid my pain.

Who So List to Hunt

SIR THOMAS WYATT

Who so list to hunt, I know where is an hind,
But as for me, helas, I may no more:
The vain travail hath wearied me so sore,
I am of them that farthest cometh behind;
Yet may I by no means my wearied mind
Draw from the deer: but as she fleeth afore,
Fainting I follow, I leave off therefore,
Since in a net I seek to hold the wind.
Who list her hunt, I put him out of doubt,
As well as I may spend his time in vain:
And, graven with diamonds, in letters plain,
There is written, her fair neck round about:
Noli me tangere, for Caesar's I am,
And wild for to hold, though I seem tame.

Song

Sir John Suckling

Why so pale and wan fond Lover?
  Prithee why so pale?
Will, when looking well can't move her,
  Looking ill prevaile?
  Prithee why so pale?

Why so dull and mute young Sinner?
  Prithee why so mute?
Will, when speaking well can't win her,
  Saying nothing doo't?
  Prithee why so mute?

Quit, quit, for shame, this will not move,
  This will not take her;
If of her selfe she will not Love,
  Nothing can make her:
  The Devill take her.

What Care I

George Wither

Shall I, wasting in despair,
Die because a woman's fair?
Or my cheeks make pale with care
'Cause another's rosy are?
Be she fairer than the day
Or the flowery meads in May—
  If she be not so to me,
    What care I how fair she be?

Shall my foolish heart be pined
'Cause I see a woman kind?
Or a well disposed nature
Joinèd with a lovely feature?
Be she meeker, kinder, than
Turtle-dove or pelican,
  If she be not so to me,
    What care I how kind she be?

Shall a woman's virtues move
Me to perish for her love?
Or her merits' value known
Make me quite forget mine own?
Be she with that goodness blest
Which may gain her name of Best;
  If she seem not such to me,
    What care I how good she be?

'Cause her fortune seems too high,
Shall I play the fool and die?
Those that bear a noble mind
Where they want of riches find,

Think what with them they would do
Who without them dare to woo;
   And unless that mind I see,
   What care I how great she be?

Great or good, or kind or fair.
I will ne'er the more despair:
If she love me, this believe,
I will die ere she shall grieve;
If she slight me when I woo,
I can scorn and let her go.
   For if she be not for me,
   What care I for whom she be?

A Woman's Looks

ANONYMOUS

A woman's looks
Are barbed hooks,
That catch by art
The strongest heart,
When yet they spend no breath.
But let them speak,
And sighing break
Forth into tears,
Their words are spears
That wound our souls to death.
The rarest wit
Is made forget,
And like a child
Is oft beguiled
With Love's sweet-seeming bait.
Love with his rod
So like a god
Commands the mind
We cannot find,
Fair shows hide foul deceit.
Time, that all things
In order brings,
Hath taught me now
To be more slow
In giving faith to speech:
Since women's words
No truth affords,
And when they kiss
They think by this
Us men to overreach.

Woman's Constancy

JOHN DONNE

Now thou hast loved me one whole day,
Tomorrow when thou leav'st, what wilt thou say?
Wilt thou then antedate some new-made vow?
  Or say that now
We are not just those persons which we were?
Or, that oaths made in reverential fear
Of Love, and his wrath, any may forswear?
Or, as true deaths true marriages untie,
So lovers' contracts, images of those,
Bind but till sleep, death's image, them unloose?
  Or, your own end to justify,
For having purposed change and falsehood, you
Can have no way but falsehood to be true?
Vain lunatic, against these 'scapes I could
  Dispute and conquer, if I would,
    Which I abstain to do,
For by tomorrow, I may think so too.

When I Was Fair and Young

Elizabeth I

When I was fair and young, then favour graced me;
Of many was I sought their mistress for to be,
But I did scorn them all, and answered them therefore:
"Go! go! go! seek some other where, importune me no more!"

How many weeping eyes, I made to pine with woe!
How many sighing hearts! I have no skill to show.
Yet I the prouder grew, and still this spake therefore:
"Go! go! go! seek some other where, importune me no more!"

Then spake fair Venus' son that proud victorious boy,
Saying: You dainty dame for that you be so coy?
I will so pluck your plumes that you shall say no more:
"Go! go! go! seek some other where, importune me no more!"

As soon as he had said, such change grew in my breast,
That neither night nor day, I could take any rest.
Then lo! I did repent that I had said before:
"Go! go! go! seek some other where, importune me no more."

To My Inconstant Mistress

Thomas Carew

When thou, poor excommunicate
  From all the joys of love, shalt see
The full reward and glorious fate
  Which my strong faith shall purchase me,
  Then curse thine own inconstancy.

A fairer hand than thine shall cure
  That heart, which thy false oaths did wound;
And to my soul a soul more pure
  Than thine shall by Love's hand be bound,
  And both with equal glory crown'd.

Then shalt thou weep, entreat, complain
  To Love, as I did once to thee;
When all thy tears shall be as vain
  As mine were then, for thou shalt be
  Damned for thy false apostasy.

In Faith, I Do Not Love Thee

WILLIAM SHAKESPEARE

In faith, I do not love thee with mine eyes,
For they in thee a thousand errors note;
But 'tis my heart that loves what they despise,
Who, in despite of view, is pleased to dote;
Nor are mine ears with thy tongue's tune delighted,
Nor tender feeling, to base touches prone,
Nor taste, nor smell, desire to be invited
To any sensual feast with thee alone:
But my five wits nor my five senses can
Dissuade one foolish heart from serving thee,
Who leaves unswayed the likeness of a man,
Thy proud heart's slave and vassal wretch to be.
   Only my plague thus far I count my gain,
   That she that makes me sin awards me pain.

To Fanny

John Keats

I cry your mercy—pity—love!—aye, love!
  Merciful love that tantalizes not,
One-thoughted, never-wandering, guileless love,
  Unmasked, and being seen—without a blot!
O! let me have thee whole,—all—all—be mine!
  That shape, that fairness, that sweet minor zest
Of love, your kiss,—those hands, those eyes divine,
  That warm, white, lucent, million-pleasured breast,—
Yourself—your soul—in pity give me all,
  Withhold no atom's atom or I die,
Or living on perhaps, your wretched thrall,
  Forget, in the mist of idle misery,
Life's purposes,—the palate of my mind
  Losing its gust, and my ambition blind!

La Belle Dame sans Merci

John Keats

Ah, what can ail thee, wretched wight,
  Alone and palely loitering;
The sedge is withered from the lake,
  And no birds sing.

Ah, what can ail thee, wretched wight,
  So haggard and so woe-begone?
The squirrel's granary is full,
  And the harvest's done.

I see a lily on thy brow,
  With anguish moist and fever dew;
And on thy cheek a fading rose
  Fast withereth too.

I met a lady in the meads
  Full beautiful, a faery's child;
Her hair was long, her foot was light,
  And her eyes were wild.

I set her on my pacing steed,
  And nothing else saw all day long;
For sideways would she lean, and sing
  A faery's song.

I made a garland for her head,
  And bracelets too, and fragrant zone;
She looked at me as she did love,
  And made sweet moan.

She found me roots of relish sweet,
  And honey wild, and manna dew;
And sure in language strange she said,
  I love thee true.

She took me to her elfin grot,
   And there she gazed and sighèd deep,
And there I shut her wild sad eyes—
   So kissed to sleep.

And there we slumbered on the moss,
   And there I dreamed, ah woe betide,
The latest dream I ever dreamed
   On the cold hill side.

I saw pale kings, and princes too,
   Pale warriors, death-pale were they all;
Who cried—"La belle Dame sans merci
   Hath thee in thrall!"

I saw their starved lips in the gloam
   With horrid warning gapèd wide,
And I awoke, and found me here
   On the cold hill side.

And this is why I sojourn here
   Alone and palely loitering,
Though the sedge is withered from the lake,
   And no birds sing.

They Flee from Me

Sir Thomas Wyatt

They flee from me, that sometime did me seek
    With naked foot, stalking in my chamber.
I have seen them gentle, tame, and meek,
    That now are wild, and do not remember
    That sometime they put themselves in danger
        To take bread at my hand; and now they range
        Busily seeking with a continual change.

Thanked be fortune it hath been otherwise
    Twenty times better; but once, in special,
In thin array, after a pleasant guise,
    When her loose gown from her shoulders did fall,
    And she me caught in her arms long and small;
        Therewith all sweetly did me kiss,
        And softly said, "Dear heart, how like you this?"

It was no dream: I lay broad waking:
    But all is turned, thorough my gentleness,
Into a strange fashion of forsaking;
    And I have leave to go of her goodness,
    And she also to use newfangleness.
        But since that I so kindly am served,
        I would fain know what she hath deserved.

On Monsieur's Departure

Elizabeth I

I grieve and dare not show my discontent;
   I love, and yet am forced to seem to hate;
I do, yet dare not say I ever meant;
   I seem stark mute, but inwardly do prate:
I am, and not: I freeze, and yet am burn'd,
Since from myself, my other self I turn'd.

My care is like my shadow in the sun,
   Follows me flying, flies when I pursue it;
Stands and lies by me, does what I have done;
   This too familiar care does make me rue it:
No means I find to rid him from my breast,
Till by the end of things it be supprest.

Some gentler passions slide into my mind,
   For I am soft and made of melting snow;
Or be more cruel, Love, and so be kind,
   Let me or float or sink, be high or low:
Or let me live with some more sweet content,
Or die, and so forget what love e'er meant.

The Lover Compareth His State to a Ship in Perilous Storm Tossed on the Sea

SIR THOMAS WYATT

My galley, charged with forgetfulness,
Thorough sharp seas in winter nights doth pass
'Tween rock and rock; and eke my foe, alas,
That is my lord, steereth with cruelness;
And every oar a thought in readiness,
As though that death were light in such a case;
An endless wind doth tear the sail apace
Of forced sighs, and trusty fearfulness;
A rain of tears, a cloud of dark disdain,
Hath done the wearied cords great hinderance;
Wreathed with error and eke with ignorance,
The stars be hid that led me to this pain.
   Drowned is reason that should me comfort,
   And I remain, despairing of the port.

Why Should Your Fair Eyes

Michael Drayton

Why should your fair eyes with such sovereign grace
Disperse their rays on every vulgar spirit,
Whilst I in darkness in the self-same place
Get not one glance to recompense my merit?
So doth the ploughman gaze the wandering star,
And only rest contented with the light,
That never learned what constellations are,
Beyond the bent of his unknowing sight,
O! why should beauty, custom to obey,
To their gross sense apply herself so ill?
Would God I were as ignorant as they,
When I am made unhappy by my skill;
Only compelled on this poor good to boast,
Heavens are not kind to them that know them most.

To a Lady that Desired I Would Love Her

Thomas Carew

Now you have freely given me leave to love,
    What will you do?
  Shall I your mirth, or passion move,
    When I begin to woo;
Will you torment, or scorn, or love me too?

Each petty beauty can disdain, and I
    Spite of your hate
  Without your leave can see, and die;
    Dispense a nobler fate!
'Tis easy to destroy, you may create.

Then give me leave to love, and love me too
    Not with design
  To raise, as Love's cursed rebels do,
    When puling poets whine,
Fame to their beauty, from their blubbered eyne.

Grief is a puddle, and reflects not clear
    Your beauty's rays;
  Joys are pure streams, your eyes appear
    Sullen in sadder lays;
In cheerful numbers they shine bright with praise,

Which shall not mention to express you fair,
    Wounds, flames, and darts,
  Storms in your brow, nets in your hair,
    Suborning all your parts,
Or to betray, or torture captive hearts.

I'll make your eyes like morning suns appear,
   As mild, and fair;
Your brow as crystal smooth, and clear,
   And your dishevelled hair
Shall flow like a calm region of the air.

Many in Aftertimes

CHRISTINA ROSSETTI

Many in aftertimes will say of you
  "He loved her"—while of me what will they say?
  Not that I loved you more than just in play,
For fashion's sake as idle women do.
Even let them prate; who know not what we knew
  Of love and parting in exceeding pain.
  Of parting hopeless here to meet again,
Hopeless on earth, and heaven is out of view.
But by my heart of love laid bare to you.
  My love that you can make not void nor vain,
Love that foregoes you but to claim anew
    Beyond this passage of the gate of death,
I charge you at the Judgment make it plain
    My love of you was life and not a breath.

Kind Are Her Answers

Thomas Campion

Kind are her answers,
But her performance keeps no day;
Breaks time, as dancers
From their own music when they stray:
All her free favors
And smooth words wing my hopes in vain.
O did ever voice so sweet but only feign?
Can true love yield such delay,
Converting joy to pain?

Lost is our freedom,
When we submit to women so:
Why do we need 'em,
When in their best they work our woe?
There is no wisdom
Can alter ends, by Fate prefixed.
O why is the good of man with evil mixed?
Never were days yet called two,
But one night went betwixt.

I Cannot Live with You

Emily Dickinson

I cannot live with you,
It would be life,
And life is over there
Behind the shelf

The sexton keeps the key to,
Putting up
Our life, his porcelain,
Like a cup

Discarded of the housewife,
Quaint or broken;
A newer Sèvres pleases,
Old ones crack.

I could not die with you,
For one must wait
To shut the other's gaze down,—
You could not.

And I, could I stand by
And see you freeze,
Without my right of frost,
Death's privilege?

Nor could I rise with you,
Because your face
Would put out Jesus',
That new grace

Glow plain and foreign
On my homesick eye,
Except that you, than he
Shone closer by.

They'd judge us—how?
For you served Heaven, you know,
Or sought to;
I could not,

Because you saturated sight,
And I had no more eyes
For sordid excellence
As Paradise.

And were you lost, I would be,
Though my name
Rang loudest
On the heavenly fame.

And were you saved,
And I condemned to be
Where you were not,
That self were hell to me.

So we must keep apart,
You there, I here,
With just the door ajar
That oceans are,
And prayer,
And that pale sustenance,
Despair!

With How Sad Steps

Sir Philip Sidney

With how sad steps, O moon, thou climb'st the skies!
How silently, and with how wan a face!
What! may it be that even in heavenly place
That busy archer his sharp arrows tries?
Sure, if that long-with-love-acquainted eyes
Can judge of love, thou feel'st a lover's case:
I read it in thy looks; thy languished grace
To me, that feel the like, thy state descries.
Then, even of fellowship, O Moon, tell me,
Is constant love deemed there but want of wit?
Are beauties there as proud as here they be?
Do they above love to be loved, and yet
　　Those lovers scorn whom that love doth possess?
　　Do they call "virtue" there—ungratefulness?

The Aged Lover Renounceth Love

Thomas, Lord Vaux

I loathe that I did love,
  In youth that I thought sweet,
As time requires for my behove,
  Methinks they are not meet.

My lusts they do me leave,
  My fancies all be fled,
And tract of time begins to weave
  Grey hairs upon my head,

For age with stealing steps
  Hath clawed me with his crutch,
And lusty life away she leaps
  As there had been none such.

My Muse doth not delight
  Me as she did before;
My hand and pen are not in plight,
  As they have been of yore.

For reason me denies
  This youthly idle rhyme;
And day by day to me she cries,
  "Leave off these toys in time."

The wrinkles in my brow,
  The furrows in my face,
Say, limping age will lodge him now
  Where youth must give him place.

The harbinger of death,
  To me I see him ride,
The cough, the cold, the gasping breath
  Doth bid me to provide

A pickaxe and a spade,
  And eke a shrouding sheet,
A house of clay for to be made
  For such a guest most meet.

Methinks I hear the clark
  That knolls the careful knell,
And bids me leave my woeful wark,
  Ere nature me compel.

My keepers knit the knot
  That youth did laugh to scorn,
Of me that clean shall be forgot
  As I had not been born.

Thus must I youth give up,
  Whose badge I long did wear;
To them I yield the wanton cup
  That better may it bear.

Lo, here the barèd skull,
  By whose bald sign I know
That stooping age away shall pull
  Which youthful years did sow.

For beauty with her band
  These crooked cares hath wrought,
And shippèd me into the land
  From whence I first was brought.

And ye that bide behind,
  Have ye none other trust:
As ye of clay were cast by kind,
  So shall ye waste to dust.

Love, That Doth Reign and Live within My Thought

HENRY HOWARD, EARL OF SURREY

Love, that doth reign and live within my thought,
And built his seat within my captive breast,
Clad in the arms wherein with me he fought,
Oft in my face he doth his banner rest.
But she that taught me to love and suffer pain,
My doubtful hope and eke my hot desire
With shamefast look to shadow and refrain,
Her smiling grace converteth straight to ire.
And coward Love, then, to the heart apace
Taketh his flight, where he doth lurk and plain,
His purpose lost, and dare not show his face.
For my lord's guilt thus faultless bide I pain,
Yet from my lord shall not my foot remove:
Sweet is the death that taketh end by love.

Wind and Window Flower

ROBERT FROST

Lovers, forget your love,
    And list to the love of these,
She a window flower,
    And he a winter breeze.

When the frosty window veil
    Was melted down at noon,
And the cagèd yellow bird
    Hung over her in tune,

He marked her through the pane,
    He could not help but mark,
And only passed her by
    To come again at dark.

He was a winter wind,
    Concerned with ice and snow,
Dead weeds and unmated birds,
    And little of love could know.

But he sighed upon the sill,
    He gave the sash a shake,
As witness all within
    Who lay that night awake.

Perchance he half prevailed
    To win her for the flight
From the firelit looking-glass
    And warm stove-window light.

But the flower leaned aside
    And thought of naught to say,
And morning found the breeze
    A hundred miles away.

The Way of It

ELLA WHEELER WILCOX

This is the way of it, wide world over,
One is beloved, and one is the lover,
  One gives and the other receives.
One lavishes all in a wild emotion,
One offers a smile for a life's devotion,
  One hopes and the other believes,
One lies awake in the night to weep,
And the other drifts off in a sweet sound sleep.

One soul is aflame with a godlike passion,
One plays with love in an idler's fashion,
  One speaks and the other hears.
One sobs, "I love you," and wet eyes show it,
And one laughs lightly, and says, "I know it,"
  With smiles for the other's tears.
One lives for the other and nothing beside,
And the other remembers the world is wide.

This is the way of it, sad earth over,
The heart that breaks is the heart of the lover,
  And the other learns to forget.
"For what is the use of endless sorrow?
Though the sun goes down, it will rise tomorrow;
  And life is not over yet."
Oh! I know this truth, if I know no other,
That passionate Love is Pain's own mother.

FAREWELL, LOVE

Since There's No Help

MICHAEL DRAYTON

Since there's no help, come let us kiss and part—
Nay, I have done, you get no more of me;
And I am glad, yea, glad with all my heart,
That thus so cleanly I myself can free.
Shake hands for ever, cancel all our vows,
And when we meet at any time again,
Be it not seen in either of our brows
That we one jot of former love retain.
Now at the last gasp of Love's latest breath,
When, his pulse failing. Passion speechless lies,
When Faith is kneeling by his bed of death,
And Innocence is closing up his eyes,
   —Now if thou would'st, when all have given him over,
   From death to life thou might'st him yet recover.

A Farewell

Coventry Patmore

With all my will, but much against my heart,
We two now part.
My Very Dear,
Our solace is, the sad road lies so clear.
It needs no art,
With faint, averted feet
And many a tear,
In our opposed paths to persevere.
Go thou to East, I West.
We will not say
There's any hope, it is so far away.
But, O, my Best,
When the one darling of our widowhead,
The nursling Grief,
Is dead,
And no dews blur our eyes
To see the peach-bloom come in evening skies,
Perchance we may,
Where now this night is day,
And even through faith of still averted feet,
Making full circle of our banishment,
Amazed meet;
The bitter journey to the bourne so sweet
Seasoning the termless feast of our content
With tears of recognition never dry.

What Does It Avail Me?

Louise Labé

Then what does it avail me, that you once
Sang so divinely of my golden hair?
And that you once, in passion could declare
That my two eyes were like two separate suns
Whose fires the god had gathered from above
To strike you down? And what of all those hot,
Distracted tears and deathless vows? And what
Was this your stratagem? That you appear
  Enslaved while you enslave me? O, my dear,
  Forgive me this suspicion! Dazed, drawn under
  By all this grief, I know not what to do
  Except once more console myself that you
  Also will grieve, wherever you may wander.

I Hid My Love

JOHN CLARE

I hid my love when young till I
Couldn't bear the buzzing of a fly;
I hid my love to my despite
Till I could not bear to look at light:
I dare not gaze upon her face
But left her memory in each place;
Where'er I saw a wild flower lie
I kissed and bade my love good-bye.

I met her in the greenest dells,
Where dewdrops pearl the wood bluebells;
The lost breeze kissed her bright blue eye,
The bee kissed and went singing by,
A sunbeam found a passage there,
A gold chain round her neck so fair;
As secret as the wild bee's song
She lay there all the summer long.

I hid my love in field and town
Till e'en the breeze would knock me down;
The bees seemed singing ballads o'er,
The fly's bass turned a lion's roar;
And even silence found a tongue,
To haunt me all the summer long;
The riddle nature could not prove
Was nothing else but secret love.

Sonnet

CHRISTINA ROSSETTI

I wish I could remember that first day,
First hour, first moment of your meeting me,
If bright or dim the season, it might be
Summer or Winter for aught that I can say;
So unrecorded did it slip away,
So blind was I to see and to foresee,
So dull to mark the budding of my tree
That would not blossom yet for many a May.
If only I could recollect it, such
A day of days! I let it come and go
As traceless as a thaw of bygone snow;
It seemed to mean so little, meant so much;
If only now I could recall that touch,
First touch of hand in hand.—Did one but know!

Down by the Salley Gardens

ANONYMOUS

Down by the salley gardens
   my love and I did meet;
She passed the salley gardens
   with little snow-white feet.
She bid me take love easy,
   as the leaves grow on the tree;
But I, being young and foolish,
   with her would not agree.

In a field by the river
   my love and I did stand,
And on my leaning shoulder
   she laid her snow-white hand.
She bid me take life easy,
   as the grass grows on the weirs;
But I was young and foolish,
   and now am full of tears.

The Look

SARA TEASDALE

Strephon kissed me in the spring,
　Robin in the fall,
But Colin only looked at me
　And never kissed at all.

Strephon's kiss was lost in jest,
　Robin's lost in play,
But the kiss in Colin's eyes
　Haunts me night and day.

Never Seek to Tell Thy Love

William Blake

Never seek to tell thy love
Love that never told can be;
For the gentle wind does move
Silently, invisibly.

I told my love, I told my ove,
I told herall my heart,
Trembling, old, in ghstly fears—
Ah, she doth depart.

Soon as she was gone from me
A traveller came by
Silently, invisibly—
O, was no deny.

From *Modern Love*

GEORGE MEREDITH

In our old shipwrecked days there was an hour,
When in the firelight steadily aglow,
Joined slackly, we beheld the red chasm grow
Among the clicking coals. Our library-bower
That eve was left to us: and hushed we sat
As lovers to whom Time is whispering.
From sudden-opened doors we heard them sing:
The nodding elders mixed good wine with chat.
Well knew we that Life's greatest treasure lay
With us, and of it was our talk. "Ah, yes!
Love dies!" I said: I never thought it less.
She yearned to me that sentence to unsay.
Then when the fire domed blackening, I found
Her cheek was salt against my kiss, and swift
Up the sharp scale of sobs her breast did lift:—
Now am I haunted by that taste! that sound!

What Should I Say

SIR THOMAS WYATT

What should I say,
　Since faith is dead,
And truth away
　From you is fled?
Should I be led
　With doubleness?
　Nay, nay, mistress!

I promised you,
　And you promised me,
To be as true,
　As I would be.
But since I see
　Your double heart,
　Farewell my part!

Though for to take
　It is not my mind,
But to forsake
　One so unkind,
And as I find
　So will I trust,
　Farewell, unjust!

Can ye say nay,
　But that you said
That I always
　Should be obeyed?
And thus betrayed,
　Or that I wist,
　Farewell, unkissed!

The Gift

SARA TEASDALE

What can I give you, my lord, my lover,
You who have given the world to me,
Showed me the light and the joy that cover
The wild sweet earth and the restless sea?

All that I have are gifts of your giving—
If I gave them again, you would find them old,
And your soul would weary of always living
Before the mirror my life would hold.

What shall I give you, my lord, my lover?
The gift that breaks the heart in me;
I bid you awake at dawn and discover
I have gone my way and left you free.

Farewell! Thou Art Too Dear

WILLIAM SHAKESPEARE

Farewell! thou art too dear for my possessing,
And like enough thou knowst thy estimate,
The Charter of thy worth gives thee releasing:
My bonds in thee are all determinate.
For how do I hold thee but by thy granting,
And for that riches where is my deserving?
The cause of this fair gift in me is wanting,
And so my patent back again is swerving.
Thy self thou gav'st, thy own worth then not knowing,
Or me to whom thou gav'st it, else mistaking,
So thy great gift upon misprision growing,
Comes home again, on better judgement making.
    Thus have I had thee as a dream doth flatter,
    In sleep a King, but waking no such matter.

Dead Love

ELIZABETH SIDDAL

Oh never weep for love that's dead
Since love is seldom true
But changes his fashion from blue to red,
From brightest red to blue,
And love was born to an early death
And is so seldom true.

Then harbour no smile on your bonny face
To win the deepest sigh.
The fairest words on truest lips
Pass on and surely die,
And you will stand alone, my dear,
When wintry winds draw nigh.

Sweet, never weep for what cannot be,
For this God has not given.
If the merest dream of love were true
Then, sweet, we should be in heaven,
And this is only earth, my dear,
Where true love is not given.

Farewell, Love

SIR THOMAS WYATT

Farewell, Love, and all thy laws forever:
Thy baited hooks shall tangle me no more;
Senec and Plato call me from thy lore,
To perfect wealth my wit for to endeavor.
In blind error when I did persevere,
Thy sharp repulse that pricketh aye so sore
Hath taught me to set in trifles no store
And scape forth, since liberty is liefer.
Therefore, farewell: go trouble younger hearts,
And in me claim no more authority;
With idle youth go use thy property
And thereon spend thy many brittle darts:
For hitherto though I have lost all my time,
Me lusteth no longer rotten boughs to climb.

The Lost Mistress

ROBERT BROWNING

All's over, then: does truth sound bitter
　　As one at first believes?
Hark, 'tis the sparrows' good-night twitter
　　About your cottage eaves!

And the leaf-buds on the vine are woolly,
　　I noticed that, today;
One day more bursts them open fully
　　—You know the red turns grey.

Tomorrow we meet the same then, dearest?
　　May I take your hand in mine?
Mere friends are we,—well, friends the merest
　　Keep much that I resign:

For each glance of the eye so bright and black,
　　Though I keep with heart's endeavour,—
Your voice, when you wish the snowdrops back,
　　Though it stay in my soul for ever!—

Yet I will but say what mere friends say,
　　Or only a thought stronger;
I will hold your hand but as long as all may,
　　Or so very little longer!

Friendship After Love

Ella Wheeler Wilcox

After the fierce midsummer all ablaze
  Has burned itself to ashes, and expires
  In the intensity of its own fires,
There come the mellow, mild, St. Martin days
Crowned with the calm of peace, but sad with haze.
  So after Love has led us, till he tires
  Of his own throes, and torments, and desires,
Comes large-eyed friendship: with a restful gaze,
He beckons us to follow, and across
  Cool verdant vales we wander free from care.
  Is it a touch of frost lies in the air?
Why are we haunted with a sense of loss?
We do not wish the pain back, or the heat;
And yet, and yet, these days are incomplete.

I Envy Not in Any Moods

ALFRED, LORD TENNYSON

I envy not in any moods
  The captive void of noble rage,
  The linnet born within the cage,
That never knew the summer woods:

I envy not the beast that takes
  His license in the field of time,
  Unfetter'd by the sense of crime,
To whom a conscience never wakes;

Nor, what may count itself as blest,
  The heart that never plighted troth,
  But stagnates in the weeds of sloth;
Nor any want-begotten rest.

I hold it true, whate'er befall;
  I feel it, when I sorrow most;
  'Tis better to have loved and lost
Than never to have loved at all.

REMEMBER ME WHEN
I AM GONE AWAY

Never the Time and the Place

ROBERT BROWNING

Never the time and the place
    And the loved one all together!
This path—how soft to pace!
    This May—what magic weather!
Where is the loved one's face?
In a dream that loved one's face meets mine,
    But the house is narrow, the place is bleak
Where, outside, rain and wind combine
    With a furtive ear, if I strive to speak,
    With a hostile eye at my flushing cheek,
With a malice that marks each word, each sign!
O enemy sly and serpentine,
Uncoil thee from the waking man!
    Do I hold the Past
    Thus firm and fast
Yet doubt if the Future hold I can?

The Taxi

Amy Lowell

When I go away from you
The world beats dead
Like a slackened drum.
I call out for you against the jutted stars
And shout into the ridges of the wind.
Streets coming fast,
One after the other,
Wedge you away from me,
And the lamps of the city prick my eyes
So that I can no longer see your face.
Why should I leave you,
To wound myself upon the sharp edges of the night?

When We Two Parted

George Gordon, Lord Byron

When we two parted
  In silence and tears,
Half broken-hearted
  To sever for years,
Pale grew the cheek and cold,
  Colder thy kiss;
Truly that hour foretold
  Sorrow to this.

The dew of the morning
  Sunk chill on my brow—
It felt like the warning
  Of what I feel now.
Thy vows are all broken,
  And light is thy fame:
I hear thy name spoken,
  And share in its shame.

They name thee before me,
  A knell to mine ear;
A shudder comes o'er me—
  Why wert thou so dear?
They know not I knew thee,
  Who knew thee too well:—
Long, long shall I rue thee,
  Too deeply to tell.

In secret we met—
  In silence I grieve,
That thy heart could forget,
  Thy spirit deceive.
If I should meet thee
  After long years,
How should I greet thee?—
  With silence and tears.

Without Her

Dante Gabriel Rossetti

What of her glass without her? The blank gray
  There where the pool is blind of the moon's face.
  Her dress without her? The tossed empty space
Of cloud-rack whence the moon has passed away.
Her paths without her? Day's appointed sway
  Usurped by desolate night. Her pillowed place
  Without her? Tears, ah me! for love's good grace,
And cold forgetfulness of night or day.

What of the heart without her? Nay, poor heart,
  Of thee what word remains ere speech be still?
  A wayfarer by barren ways and chill,
Steep ways and weary, without her thou art,
Where the long cloud, the long wood's counterpart,
  Sheds doubled darkness up the labouring hill.

Mariana

Alfred, Lord Tennyson

> Mariana in the moated grange.
> —*Measure for Measure*

With blackest moss the flower-pots
    Were thickly crusted, one and all:
The rusted nails fell from the knots
    That held the pear to the gable-wall.
The broken sheds look'd sad and strange:
    Unlifted was the clinking latch;
    Weeded and worn the ancient thatch
Upon the lonely moated grange.
    She only said, "My life is dreary,
        He cometh not," she said;
    She said, "I am aweary, aweary,
        I would that I were dead!"

Her tears fell with the dews at even;
    Her tears fell ere the dews were dried;
She could not look on the sweet heaven,
    Either at morn or eventide.
After the flitting of the bats,
    When thickest dark did trance the sky,
    She drew her casement-curtain by,
And glanced athwart the glooming flats.
    She only said, "The night is dreary,
        He cometh not," she said;
    She said, "I am aweary, aweary,
        I would that I were dead!"

Upon the middle of the night,
    Waking she heard the night-fowl crow:
The cock sung out an hour ere light:
    From the dark fen the oxen's low

Came to her: without hope of change,
    In sleep she seem'd to walk forlorn,
    Till cold winds woke the gray-eyed morn
About the lonely moated grange.
    She only said, "The day is dreary,
        He cometh not," she said;
    She said, "I am aweary, aweary,
        I would that I were dead!"

About a stone-cast from the wall
    A sluice with blacken'd waters slept,
And o'er it many, round and small,
    The cluster'd marish-mosses crept.
Hard by a poplar shook alway,
    All silver-green with gnarled bark:
    For leagues no other tree did mark
The level waste, the rounding gray.
    She only said, "My life is dreary,
        He cometh not," she said;
    She said, "I am aweary, aweary,
        I would that I were dead!"

And ever when the moon was low,
    And the shrill winds were up and away,
In the white curtain, to and fro,
    She saw the gusty shadow sway.
But when the moon was very low,
    And wild winds bound within their cell,
    The shadow of the poplar fell
Upon her bed, across her brow.
    She only said, "The night is dreary,
        He cometh not," she said;
    She said, "I am aweary, aweary,
        I would that I were dead!"

All day within the dreamy house,
   The doors upon their hinges creak'd;
The blue fly sung in the pane; the mouse
   Behind the mouldering wainscot shriek'd,

Or from the crevice peer'd about.
   Old faces glimmer'd thro' the doors,
   Old footsteps trod the upper floors,
Old voices called her from without.
   She only said, "My life is dreary,
      He cometh not," she said;
   She said, "I am aweary, aweary,
      I would that I were dead!"

The sparrow's chirrup on the roof,
   The slow clock ticking, and the sound
Which to the wooing wind aloof
   The poplar made, did all confound
Her sense; but most she loathed the hour
   When the thick-moted sunbeam lay
   Athwart the chambers, and the day
Was sloping toward his western bower.
   Then, said she, "I am very dreary,
      He will not come," she said;
   She wept, "I am aweary, aweary,
      Oh God, that I were dead!"

Going to the Wars

RICHARD LOVELACE

Tell me not (Sweet) I am unkind,
  That from the nunnery
Of thy chaste breast, and quiet mind,
  To war and arms I fly.

True; a new mistress now I chase,
  The first foe in the field;
And with a stronger faith embrace
  A sword, a horse, a shield.

Yet this inconstancy is such,
  As you too shall adore;
I could not love thee (Dear) so much,
  Loved I not honour more.

To Althea from Prison

RICHARD LOVELACE

When Love with unconfinèd wings
  Hovers within my gates;
And my divine Althea brings
  To whisper at the grates:
When I lie tangled in her hair,
  And fettered to her eye;
The birds, that wanton in the air,
  Know no such liberty.

When flowing cups run swiftly round
  With no allaying Thames,
Our careless heads with roses bound,
  Our hearts with loyal flames;
When thirsty grief in wine we steep,
  When healths and draughts go free,
Fishes that tipple in the deep,
  Know no such liberty.

When (like committed linnets) I
  With shriller throat shall sing
The sweetness, mercy, majesty,
  And glories of my King;
When I shall voice aloud, how good
  He is, how great should be;
Enlargèd winds that curl the flood,
  Know no such liberty.

Stone walls do not a prison make,
  Nor iron bars a cage;
Minds innocent and quiet take
  That for an hermitage;
If I have freedom in my Love,
  And in my soul am free;
Angels alone that soar above,
  Enjoy such liberty.

Remember Me When I Am Gone Away

CHRISTINA ROSSETTI

Remember me when I am gone away,
  Gone far away into the silent land;
  When you can no more hold me by the hand,
Nor I half turn to go, yet turning stay.
Remember me when no more day by day
  You tell me of our future that you planned:
  Only remember me; you understand
It will be late to counsel then or pray.

Yet if you should forget me for a while
  And afterwards remember, do not grieve:
  For if the darkness and corruption leave
A vestige of the thoughts that once I had,
Better by far you should forget and smile
  Than that you should remember and be sad.

To —

PERCY BYSSHE SHELLEY

Music, when soft voices die,
Vibrates in the memory—
Odours, when sweet violets sicken,
Live within the sense they quicken.

Rose leaves, when the rose is dead,
Are heaped for the beloved's bed;
And so thy thoughts, when thou art gone,
Love itself shall slumber on.

She Dwelt Among the Untrodden Ways

William Wordsworth

She dwelt among the untrodden ways
  Beside the springs of Dove,

A maid whom there were none to praise
  And very few to love:

A violet by a mossy stone
  Half hidden from the eye!
—Fair as a star, when only one
  Is shining in the sky.

She lived unknown, and few could know
  When Lucy ceased to be;
But she is in her grave, and, oh,
  The difference to me!

Surprised by Joy

WILLIAM WORDSWORTH

I turned to share the transport—Oh! with whom
But Thee, deep buried in the silent tomb.
That spot which no vicissitude can find?
Love, faithful love, recalled thee to my mind—
But how could I forget thee Through what power,
Even for the least division of an hour,
Have I been so beguiled as to be blind
To my most grievous loss!—That thought's return
Was the worst pang that sorrow ever bore,
Save one, one only, when I stood forlorn,
Knowing my heart's best treasure was no more;
That neither present time, nor years inborn
Could to my sight that heavenly face restore.

I Have Led Her Home, My Love

Alfred, Lord Tennyson

I have led her home, my love, my only friend,
There is none like her, none.
And never yet so warmly ran my blood
And sweetly, on and on
Calming itself to the long-wished-for end,
Full to the banks, close on the promised good.

None like her, none.
Just now the dry-tongued laurels' pattering talk
Seem'd her light foot along the garden walk,
And shook my heart to think she comes once more;
But even then I heard her close the door,
The gates of Heaven are closed, and she is gone.

There is none like her, none.
Nor will be when our summers have deceased.
O, art thou sighing for Lebanon
In the long breeze that streams to thy delicious East,
Sighing for Lebanon,
Dark cedar, tho' thy limbs have here increased,
Upon a pastoral slope as fair,

And looking to the South, and fed
With honeyed rain and delicate air,
And haunted by the starry head
Of her whose gentle will has changed my fate,
And made my life a perfumed altar-frame;
And over whom thy darkness must have spread
With such delight as theirs of old, thy great
Forefathers of the thornless garden, there
Shadowing the snow-limbed Eve from whom she came.

Here will I lie, while these long branches sway,
And you fair stars that crown a happy day
Go in and out as if at merry play,
Who am no more so all forlorn,
As when it seemed far better to be born
To labour and the mattock-hardened hand
Than nursed at ease and brought to understand
A sad astrology, the boundless plan
That makes you tyrants in your iron skies,
Innumerable, pitiless, passionless eyes,
Cold fires, yet with power to burn and brand
His nothingness into man.

But now shine on, and what care I,
Who in this stormy gulf have found a pearl
The countercharm of space and hollow sky,
And do accept my madness, and would die
To save from some slight shame one simple girl.

Would die; for sullen-seeming Death may give
More life to Love than is or ever was
In our low world, where yet 'tis sweet to live.
Let no one ask me how it came to pass;
It seems that I am happy, that to me
A livelier emerald twinkles in the grass,
A purer sapphire melts into the sea.

Not die; but live a life of truest breath,
And teach true life to fight with mortal wrongs.
Oh, why should Love, like men in drinking-songs,
Spice his fair banquet with the dust of death?

Make answer, Maud my bliss,
Maud made my Maud by that long loving kiss,
Life of my life, wilt thou not answer this?
"The dusky strand of Death inwoven here
With dear Love's tie, makes Love himself more dear."

Is that enchanted moan only the swell
Of the long waves that roll in yonder bay?
And hark the clock within, the silver knell
Of twelve sweet hours that past in bridal white,
And die to live, long as my pulses play;
But now by this my love has closed her sight
And given false death her hand, and stol'n away
To dreamful wastes where footless fancies dwell

Among the fragments of the golden day.
May nothing there her maiden grace affright!
Dear heart, I feel with thee the drowsy spell.
My bride to be, my evermore delight,
My own heart's heart, my ownest own, farewell;
It is but for a little space I go:
And ye meanwhile far over moor and fell
Beat to the noiseless music of the night!
Has our whole earth gone nearer to the glow
Of your soft splendour that you look so bright?
I have climbed nearer out of lonely Hell.
Beat, happy stars, timing with things below,
Beat with my heart more blest than heart can tell.
Blest, but for some dark undercurrent woe
That seems to draw—but it shall not be so:
Let all be well, be well.

Somewhere or Other

Christina Rossetti

Somewhere or other there must surely be
  The face not seen, the voice not heard,
The heart that not yet—never yet—ah me!
  Made answer to my word.

Somewhere or other, may be near or far;
  Past land and sea, clean out of sight;
Beyond the wandering moon, beyond the star
  That tracks her night by night.

Somewhere or other, may be far or near;
  With just a wall, a hedge, between;
With just the last leaves of the dying year
  Fallen on a turf grown green.

Complaint of the Absence of Her Lover Being Upon the Sea

Henry Howard, Earl of Surrey

O happy dames, that may embrace
  The fruit of your delight,
Help to bewail the woeful case
  And eke the heavy plight
Of me, that wonted to rejoice
The fortune of my pleasant choice;
Good ladies, help to fill my mourning voice.

In ship, freight with rememberance
  Of thoughts and pleasures past,
He sails that hath in governance
  My life while it will last;
With scalding sighs, for lack of gale,
Furthering his hope, that is his sail,
Toward me, the sweet port of his avail.

Alas! how oft in dreams I see
  Those eyes that were my food;
Which sometime so delighted me,
  That yet they do me good;
Wherewith I wake with his return,
Whose absent flame did make me burn:
But when I find the lack, Lord, how I mourn!

When other lovers in arms across
  Rejoice their chief delight.
Drowned in tears, to mourn my loss
  I stand the bitter night
In my window, where I may see
Before the winds how the clouds flee.
Lo! what a mariner love hath made me!

And in green waves when the salt flood
  Doth rise by rage of wind,
A thousand fancies in that mood
  Assail my restless mind.
Alas! now drencheth my sweet foe,
That with the spoil of my heart did go,
And left me; but, alas! why did he so?

And when the seas wax calm again
  To chase fro me annoy,
My doubtful hope doth cause me plain;
  So dread cuts off my joy.
Thus is my wealth mingled with woe,
And of each thought a doubt doth grow;
"Now he comes! Will he come? Alas, no, no!"

A Letter to Her Husband, Absent Upon Public Employment

ANNE BRADSTREET

My head, my heart, mine Eyes, my life, nay more,
My joy, my Magazine of earthly store,
If two be one, as surely thou and I,
How stayest thou there, whilst I at *Ipswich* lye?
So many steps, head from the heart to sever
If but a neck, soon should we be together:
I like the earth this season, mourn in black,
My Sun is gone so far in's Zodiack,
Whom whilst I 'joy'd, nor storms, nor frosts I felt,
His warmth such frigid colds did cause to melt.
My chilled limbs now nummed lye forlorn;
Return, return sweet *Sol* from *Capricorn*;
In this dead time, alas, what can I more
Than view those fruits which through thy heat I bore?
Which sweet contentment yield me for a space,
True living Pictures of their Fathers face.
O strange effect! now thou art *Southward* gone,
I weary grow, the tedious day so long;
But when thou *Northward* to me shalt return,
I wish my Sun may never set, but burn
Within the Cancer of my glowing breast,
The welcome house of him my dearest guest.
Where ever, ever stay, and go not thence,
Till natures sad decree shall call thee hence;
Flesh of thy flesh, bone of thy bone,
I here, thou there, yet both but one.

How Like a Winter Hath My Absence Been

WILLIAM SHAKESPEARE

How like a winter hath my absence been
From thee, the pleasure of the fleeting year!
What freezings have I felt, what dark days seen!
What old December's bareness everywhere!
And yet this time removed was summer's time,
The teeming autumn, big with rich increase,
Bearing the wanton burden of the prime,
Like widowed wombs after their lords' decease:
Yet this abundant issue seemed to me
But hope of orphans and unfathered fruit;
For summer and his pleasures wait on thee,
And, thou away, the very birds are mute,
   Or, if they sing, 'tis with so dull a cheer,
   That leaves look pale, dreading the winter's near.

Echo

Christina Rossetti

Come to me in the silence of the night;
    Come in the speaking silence of a dream;
Come with soft rounded cheeks and eyes as bright
        As sunlight on a stream;
            Come back in tears,
O memory, hope, love of finished years.

Oh dream how sweet, too sweet, too bitter sweet,
    Whose wakening should have been in Paradise,
Where souls brimfull of love abide and meet;
        Where thirsting longing eyes
            Watch the slow door
That opening, letting in, lets out no more.

Yet come to me in dreams, that I may live
    My very life again tho' cold in death:
Come back to me in dreams, that I may give
        Pulse for pulse, breath for breath:
            Speak low, lean low,
As long ago, my love, how long ago.

A Song

Lizette Woodworth Reese

Oh, Love, he went a-straying,
A long time ago!
I missed him in the Maying,
When blossoms were of snow;
So back I came by the old sweet way;
And for I loved him so, wept that he came not with me,
A long time ago!
Wide open stood my chamber door,
And one stepped forth to greet;
Gray Grief, strange Grief, who turned me sore
With words he spake so sweet.
I gave him meat; I gave him drink;
(And listened for Love's feet.)
How many years? I cannot think;
In truth, I do not know—
Ah, long time ago!
Oh, Love, he came not back again,
Although I kept me fair;
And each white May, in field and lane,
I waited for him there!
Yea, he forgot; but Grief stayed on,
And in Love's empty chair
Doth sit and tell of days long gone—
'Tis more than I can bear!

A Dirge

Christina Rossetti

Why were you born when the snow was falling?
You should have come to the cuckoo's calling,
Or when grapes are green in the cluster,
Or, at least, when lithe swallows muster
  For their far off flying
  From summer dying.

Why did you die when the lambs were cropping?
You should have died at the apples' dropping,
When the grasshopper comes to trouble,
And the wheat-fields are sodden stubble,
  And all winds go sighing
  For sweet things dying.

Annabel Lee

Edgar Allan Poe

It was many and many a year ago,
    In a kingdom by the sea,
That a maiden there lived whom you may know
    By the name of Annabel Lee;
And this maiden she lived with no other thought
    Than to love and be loved by me.

I was a child and she was a child,
    In this kingdom by the sea;
But we loved with a love that was more than love—
    I and my Annabel Lee;
With a love that the winged seraphs of heaven
    Coveted her and me.

And this was the reason that, long ago,
    In this kingdom by the sea,
A wind blew out of a cloud, chilling
    My beautiful Annabel Lee;
So that her highborn kinsman came
    And bore her away from me,
To shut her up in a sepulchre
    In this kingdom by the sea.

The angels, not half so happy in heaven,
    Went envying her and me—
Yes!—that was the reason (as all men know,
    In this kingdom by the sea)
That the wind came out of the cloud by night,
    Chilling and killing my Annabel Lee.

But our love it was stronger by far than the love
  Of those who were older than we—
  Of many far wiser than we—
And neither the angels in heaven above,
  Nor the demons down under the sea,
Can ever dissever my soul from the soul
  Of the beautiful Annabel Lee.

For the moon never beams without bringing me dreams
  Of the beautiful Annabel Lee;
And the stars never rise but I feel the bright eyes
  Of the beautiful Annabel Lee;
And so, all the night-tide, I lie down by the side
Of my darling—my darling—my life and my bride,
  In the sepulchre there by the sea,
  In her tomb by the sounding sea.

O That 'Twere Possible

ALFRED, LORD TENNYSON

O that 'twere possible
After long grief and pain
To find the arms of my true love
Round me once again! . . .

A shadow flits before me,
Not thou, but like to thee:
Ah, Christ! that it were possible
For one short hour to see
The souls we loved, that they might tell us
What and where they be!

Remembrance

Emily Brontë

Cold in the earth—and the deep snow piled above thee!
Far, far removed, cold in the dreary grave!
Have I forgot, my only Love, to love thee,
Severed at last by Time's all-severing wave?

Now, when alone, do my thoughts no longer hover
Over the mountains, on that northern shore,
Resting their wings where heath and fern leaves cover
Thy noble heart forever, ever more?

Cold in the earth—and fifteen wild Decembers,
From those brown hills, have melted into spring;
Faithful, indeed, is the spirit that remembers
After such years of change and suffering!

Sweet Love of youth, forgive, if I forget thee,
While the world's tide is bearing me along:
Other desires and other hopes beset me,
Hopes which obscure but cannot do thee wrong!

No later light has lightened up my heaven,
No second morn has ever shone for me;
All my life's bliss from thy dear life was given,
All my life's bliss is in the grave with thee.

But when the days of golden dreams had perished,
And even Despair was powerless to destroy,
Then did I learn how existence could be cherished,
Strengthened, and fed without the aid of joy.

Then did I check the tears of useless passion—
Weaned my young soul from yearning after thine;
Sternly denied its burning wish to hasten
Down to that tomb already more than mine!

And, even yet, I dare not let it languish,
Dare not indulge in memory's rapturous pain;
Once drinking deep of that divinest anguish,
How could I seek the empty world again?

If You Were Coming in the Fall

EMILY DICKINSON

If you were coming in the fall,
I'd brush the summer by
With half a smile and half a spurn,
As housewives do a fly.

If I could see you in a year,
I'd wind the months in balls,
And put them each in separate drawers,
Until their time befalls.

If only centuries delayed,
I'd count them on my hand,
Subtracting till my fingers dropped
Into Van Diemen's Land.

If certain, when this life was out,
That yours and mine should be,
I'd toss it yonder like a rind,
And taste eternity.

But now, all ignorant of the length
Of time's uncertain wing,
It goads me, like the goblin bee,
That will not state its sting.

Tides

HELEN HUNT JACKSON

O patient shore, that canst not go to meet
Thy love, the restless sea, how comfortest
Thou all thy loneliness? Art thou at rest,
When, loosing his strong arms from round thy feet,
He turns away? Know'st thou, however sweet
That other shore may be, that to thy breast
He must return? And when in sterner test
He folds thee to a heart which does not beat,
Wraps thee in ice, and gives no smile, no kiss,
To break long wintry days, still dost thou miss
Naught from thy trust? Still wait, unfaltering,
The higher, warmer waves which leap in spring?
O sweet, wise shore, to be so satisfied!
O heart, learn from the shore! Love has a tide!

A Red, Red Rose

Robert Burns

O, my luve is like a red red rose
That's newly sprung in June:
O, my luve is like the melodie
That's sweetly played in tune.

As fair art thou, my bonie lass,
So deep in luve am I;
And I will luve thee still, my dear,
Till a' the seas gang dry.

Till a' the seas gang dry, my dear,
And the rocks melt wi' the sun;
And I will luve thee still, my dear,
While the sands o' life shall run.

And fare thee weel, my only luve!
And fare thee weel a while!
And I will come again, my luve,
Tho' it were ten thousand mile.

Western Wind

ANONYMOUS

Western wind, when will thou blow,
The small rain down can rain?
Christ, if my love were in my arms
And I in my bed again!

MY TRUE LOVE
HATH MY HEART

My True Love Hath My Heart

SIR PHILIP SIDNEY

My true Love hath my heart, and I have his,
By just exchange one for the other given:
I hold his dear, and mine he cannot miss;
There never was a better bargain driven.
His heart in me keeps me and him in one,
My heart in him his thoughts and senses guides:
He loves my heart, for once it was his own;
I cherish his because in me it bides.
His heart his wound receivèd from my sight,
My heart was wounded with his wounded heart;
For as from me, on him his hurt did light,
So still methought in me his hurt did smart.
Both, equal hurt, in this change sought our bliss:
My true Love hath my heart, and I have his.

Love Me Little, Love Me Long

Anonymous

Love me little, love me long,
Is the burden of my song.
Love that is too hot and strong
    Burneth soon to waste:
Still, I would not have thee cold,
Not too backward, nor too bold;
Love that lasteth till 'tis old
    Fadeth not in haste.
      Love me little, love me long,
      Is the burden of my song.

If thou lovest me too much,
It will not prove as true as touch;
Love me little, more than such,
    For I fear the end:
I am with little well content,
And a little from thee sent
Is enough, with true intent
    To be steadfast friend.
      Love me little, love me long,
      Is the burden of my song.

Say thou lov'st me while thou live;
I to thee my love will give,
Never dreaming to deceive
    Whiles that life endures:
Nay, and after death, in sooth,
I too thee will keep my truth,
As now, when in my May of youth:
    This my love assures.
      Love me little, love me long,
      Is the burden of my song.

Constant love is moderate ever,
And it will through life persèver:
Give me that, with true endeavour
   I will it restore.
A suit of durance let it be
For all weathers that for me,
For the land or for the sea,
   Lasting evermore.
     Love me little, love me long,
     Is the burden of my song.

Winter's cold, or summer's heat,
Autumn's tempests, on it beat,
It can never know defeat,
   Never can rebel:
Such the love that I would gain,
Such the love, I tell thee plain,
Thou must give, or woo in vain:
   So to thee, farewell
     Love me little, love me long,
     Is the burden of my song.

From *Amoretti*

EDMUND SPENSER

One day I wrote her name upon the strand,
But came the waves and washéd it away:
Agayne I wrote it with a second hand,
But came the tyde, and made my pains his pray.
"Vayne man," sayd she, "that doest in vaine assay,
A mortall thing so to immortalize,
For I my selve shall lyke to this decay,
And eek my name bee wypéd out lykewize."
"Not so," quod I, "let baser things devize
To dy in dust, but you shall live by fame:
My verse your vertues rare shall eternize,
And in the hevens wryte your glorious name.
Where whenas death shall all the world subdew,
Our love shall live, and later life renew."

A Face That Should Content Me Wonderous Well

Sir Thomas Wyatt

A face that should content me wonderous well
Should not be fair but lovely to behold,
With gladsome cheer all grief for to expel;
With sober looks so would I that it should
Speak without words such words as none can tell;
Her tress also should be of crisped gold;
With wit: and thus might chance I might be tied,
And knit again the knot that should not slide.

To Asra

Samuel Taylor Coleridge

Are there two things, of all which men possess,
That are so like each other and so near,
As mutual Love seems like to Happiness?
Dear Asra, woman beyond utterance dear!
This Love which ever welling at my heart,
Now in its living fount doth heave and fall,
Now overflowing pours thro' every part
Of all my frame, and fills and changes all,
Like vernal waters springing up through snow,
This Love that seeming great beyond the power
Of growth, yet seemeth ever more to grow,
Could I transmute the whole to one rich Dower
Of Happy Life, and give it all to Thee,
Thy lot, methinks, were Heaven, thy age, Eternity!

Sonnet from the Portuguese VI

ELIZABETH BARRETT BROWNING

Go from me. Yet I feel that I shall stand
Henceforward in thy shadow. Nevermore
Alone upon the threshold of my door
Of individual life, I shall command
The uses of my soul, nor lift my hand
Serenely in the sunshine as before,
Without the sense of that which I forbore, . .
Thy touch upon the palm. The widest land
Doom takes to part us, leaves thy heart in mine
With pulses that beat double. What I do
And what I dream include thee, as the wine
Must taste of its own grapes. And when I sue
God for myself, He hears that name of thine,
And sees within my eyes, the tears of two.

Silent Noon

Dante Gabriel Rossetti

Your hands lie open in the long fresh grass,—
   The finger-points look through like rosy blooms:
   Your eyes smile peace. The pasture gleams and glooms
'Neath billowing skies that scatter and amass.
All round our nest, far as the eye can pass,
   Are golden kingcup-fields with silver edge
   Where the cow-parsley skirts the hawthorn-hedge.
'Tis visible silence, still as the hour-glass.

Deep in the sun-searched growths the dragon-fly
Hangs like a blue-thread loosened from the sky:—
   So this wing'd hour is dropt to us from above.
Oh! clasp we to our hearts, for deathless dower,
This close-companioned inarticulate hour
   When two-fold silence was the song of love.

Love's Growth

John Donne

I scarce believe my love to be so pure
  As I had thought it was,
   Because it doth endure
Vicissitude, and season, as the grass;
Methinks I lied all winter, when I swore
My love was infinite, if spring make' it more.

But if medicine, love, which cures all sorrow
With more, not only be no quintessence,
But mixed of all stuffs paining soul or sense,
And of the sun his working vigor borrow,
Love's not so pure, and abstract, as they use
To say, which have no mistress but their muse,
But as all else, being elemented too,
Love sometimes would contemplate, sometimes do.

And yet no greater, but more eminent,
  Love by the spring is grown;
   As, in the firmament,
Stars by the sun are not enlarged, but shown,
Gentle love deeds, as blossoms on a bough,
From love's awakened root do bud out now.

If, as water stirred more circles be
Produced by one, love such additions take,
Those, like so many spheres, but one heaven make,
For they are all concentric unto thee;
And though each spring do add to love new heat,
As princes do in time of action get
New taxes, and remit them not in peace,
No winter shall abate the spring's increase.

The Lady's Yes

Elizabeth Barrett Browning

I

"Yes," I answered you last night;
"No," this morning, sir, I say.
Colors seen by candlelight
Will not look the same by day.

II

When the viols played their best,
Lamps above and laughs below,
Love me sounded like a jest,
Fit for *yes* or fit for *no*.

III

Call me false or call me free—
Vow, whatever light may shine,
No man on your face shall see
Any grief for change on mine.

IV

Yet the sin is on us both;
Time to dance is not to woo;
Wooing light makes fickle troth,
Scorn of *me* recoils on *you*.

V

Learn to win a lady's faith
Nobly as the thing is high,
Bravely, as for life and death—
With a loyal gravity.

VI

Lead her from the festive boards,
 Point her to the starry skies;
Guard her, by your truthful words,
 Pure from courtship's flatteries.

VII

By your truth she shall be true,
 Ever true, as wives of yore;
And her *yes*, once said to you,
 shall be Yes for evermore.

I Shall Be Married on Monday Morning

Anonymous

As I was walking one morning in spring,
I heard a fair maiden most charmingly sing,
All under her cow, as she sat a-milking,
Saying, I shall be married, next Monday morning.

You fairest of all creatures, my eyes e'er beheld,
Oh! where do you live love, or where do you dwell,
I dwell at the top of yon bonny brown hill,
I shall be fifteen years old next Monday morning.

Fifteen years old love, is too young to marry,
The other five years love, I'd have you to tarry,
And perhaps in the meantime love you might be sorry,
So put back your wedding, next Monday morning.

You talk like a man without reason or skill,
Five years I've been waiting against my will,
Now, I am resolved my mind to fulfil,
I wish that tomorrow was Monday morning.

On Saturday night it is all my care,
To powder my locks and curl my hair,
And my two pretty maidens to wait on me there,
To dance at my wedding next Monday morning.

My husband will buy me a guinea gold ring,
And at night he'll give me a far better thing,
With two precious jewels he'll be me adorning,
When I am his bride, on Monday morning.

Wedding Hymn

Sidney Lanier

Thou God, whose high, eternal Love
Is the only blue sky of our life,
Clear all the Heaven that bends above
The life-road of this man and wife.
May these two lives be but one note
In the world's strange-sounding harmony,
Whose sacred music e'er shall float
Through every discord up to Thee.
As when from separate stars two beams
Unite to form one tender ray:
As when two sweet but shadowy dreams
Explain each other in the day:
So may these two dear hearts one light
Emit, and each interpret each.
Let an angel come and dwell tonight
In this dear double-heart, and teach.

Bridal Song

George Chapman

O come, soft rest of cares! come, Night!
  Come, naked Virtue's only tire,
The reapèd harvest of the light
  Bound up in sheaves of sacred fire,
    Love calls to war:
      Sighs his alarms,
    Lips his swords are,
      The field his arms.

Come, Night, and lay thy velvet hand
  On glorious Day's outfacing face;
And all thy crownèd flames command
  For torches to our nuptial grace.
    Love calls to war:
      Sighs his alarms,
    Lips his swords are,
      The field his arms.

Marriage Morning

Alfred, Lord Tennyson

Light, so low upon earth,
    You send a flash to the sun.
Here is the golden close of love,
    All my wooing is done.
Oh, the woods and the meadows,
    Woods, where we hid from the wet,
Stiles where we stayed to be kind,
    Meadows in which we met!
Light, so low in the vale
    You flash and lighten afar,
For this is the golden morning of love,
    And you are his morning star.
Flash, I am coming, I come,
    By meadow and stile and wood,
Oh, lighten into my eyes and my heart,
    Into my heart and my blood!
Heart, are you great enough
    For a love that never tires?
O heart, are you great enough for love?
    I have heard of thorns and briers.
Over the thorns and briers,
    Over the meadows and stiles,
Over the world to the end of it
    Flash for a million miles.

The Real and True and Sure

ROBERT BROWNING

Marriage on earth seems such a counterfeit,
Mere imitation of the inimitable:
In heaven we have the real and true and sure.
'Tis there they neither marry nor are given
In marriage but are as the angels: right,
Oh how right that is, how like Jesus Christ
To say that! Marriage-making for the earth,
With gold so much,—birth, power, repute so much,
Or beauty, youth so much, in lack of these!
Be as the angels rather, who, apart,
Know themselves into one, are found at length
Married, but marry never, no, nor give
In marriage; they are man and wife at once
When the true time is: here we have to wait
Not so long neither! Could we by a wish
Have what we will and get the future now,
Would we wish aught done undone in the past?
So, let him wait God's instant men call years;
Meantime hold hard by truth and his great soul,
Do out the duty! Through such souls alone
God stooping shows sufficient of His light
For us i' the dark to rise by. And I rise.

The Good Morrow

John Donne

I wonder by my troth, what thou and I
　　Did, till we loved? were we not weaned till then?
But sucked on country pleasures, childishly?
　　Or snorted we i'the seven sleepers' den?
'Twas so; But this, all pleasures fancies be.
If ever any beauty I did see,
Which I desired, and got, 'twas but a dream of thee.

And now good morrow to our waking souls,
　　Which watch not one another out of fear;
For love, all love of other sights controls,
　　And makes one little room, an everywhere.
Let sea-discoverers to new worlds have gone,
Let maps to others, worlds on worlds have shown,
Let us possess our world, each hath one, and is one.

My face in thine eye, thine in mine appears,
　　And true plain hearts do in the faces rest,
Where can we find two better hemispheres
　　Without sharp North, without declining West?
Whatever dies, was not mixed equally;
If our two loves be one, or, thou and I
Love so alike, that none do slacken, none can die.

The Anniversary

John Donne

All kings, and all their favourites,
  All glory of honours, beauties, wits,
The sun itself, which makes times, as they pass,
Is elder by a year, now, than it was

When thou and I first one another saw:
All other things to their destruction draw,
  Only our love hath no decay;
This, no tomorrow hath, nor yesterday;
Running, it never runs from us away,
But truly keeps his first, last, everlasting day.

  Two graves must hide thine and my corse,
  If one might, death were no divorce.
Alas, as well as other princes, we
(Who prince enough in one another be)
Must leave at last in death, these eyes, and ears,
Oft fed with true oaths, and with sweet salt tears;
  But souls where nothing dwells but love
(All other thoughts being inmates) then shall prove
This, or a love increasèd there above,
When bodies to their graves, souls from their graves remove.

  And then we shall be throughly blest,
  But we no more than all the rest;
Here upon earth, we are kings, and none but we
Can be such kings, nor of such subjects be.
Who is so safe as we? where none can do
Treason to us, except one of us two.
  True and false fears let us refrain.
Let us love nobly, and live, and add again
Years and years unto years, till we attain
To write threescore: this is the second of our reign.

O! Never Say That I Was False of Heart

WILLIAM SHAKESPEARE

O! never say that I was false of heart,
Though absence seemed my flame to qualify.
As easy might I from myself depart
As from my soul, which in thy breast doth lie:
That is my home of love; if I have ranged,
Like him that travels. I return again,
Just to the time, not with the time exchanged,
So that myself bring water for my stain.
Never believe, though in my nature reigned
All frailties that besiege all kinds of blood,
That it could so preposterously be stained,
To leave for nothing all thy sum of good;
   For nothing this wide universe I call,
    Save thou, my rose; in it thou art my all.

Sonnet from the Portuguese XIV

ELIZABETH BARRETT BROWNING

If thou must love me, let it be for nought
Except for love's sake only. Do not say
"I love her for her smile—her look—her way
Of speaking gently, . . . for a trick of thought
That falls in well with mine, and certes brought
A sense of pleasant ease on such a day"—
For these things in themselves, Belovèd, may
Be changed, or change for thee,—and love, so wrought.
May be unwrought so. Neither love me for
Thine own dear pity's wiping my cheeks dry,—
A creature might forget to weep, who bore
Thy comfort long, and lose thy love thereby!
But love me for love's sake, that evermore
Thou may'st love on, through love's eternity.

A Valediction: Forbidding Mourning

John Donne

As virtuous men pass mildly away,
    And whisper to their souls, to go,
Whilst some of their sad friends do say,
    The breath goes now, and some say, no:

So let us melt, and make no noise,
    No tear-floods, nor sigh-tempests move,
T'were profanation of our joys
    To tell the laity our love.

Moving of th'earth brings harms and fears,
    Men reckon what it did and meant,
But trepidation of the spheres,
    Though greater far, is innocent.

Dull sublunary lovers' love
    (Whose soul is sense) cannot admit
Absence, because it doth remove
    Those things which elemented it.

But we by a love, so much refined
    That our selves know not what it is,
Inter-assurèd of the mind.
    Care less, eyes, lips, and hands to miss.

Our two souls therefore, which are one,
    Though I must go, endure not yet
A breach, but an expansion,
    Like gold to airy thinness beat.

If they be two, they are two so
  As stiff twin compasses are two,
Thy soul, the fixt foot, makes no show
  To move, but doth, if th' other do.

And though it in the center sit,
  Yet when the other far doth roam,
It leans, and hearkens after it,
  And grows erect, as that comes home.

Such wilt thou be to me, who must
  Like th' other foot, obliquely run;
Thy firmness makes my circle just,
  And makes me end, where I begun.

Sonnet from the Portuguese XLIII

Elizabeth Barrett Browning

How do I love thee? Let me count the ways.
I love thee to the depth and breadth and height
My soul can reach, when feeling out of sight
For the ends of Being and ideal Grace.
I love thee to the level of every day's
Most quiet need, by sun and candle light.
I love thee freely, as men strive for Right;
I love thee purely, as they turn from Praise.
I love thee with the passion put to use
In my old griefs, and with my childhood's faith.
I love thee with a love I seemed to lose
With my lost saints—I love thee with the breath,
Smiles, tears, of all my life—and, if God choose,
I shall but love thee better after death.

The Long Love

Sir Thomas Wyatt

The long love that in my thought doth harbour,
And in mine heart doth keep his residence,
Into my face presseth with bold pretence,
And therein campeth, spreading his banner.
She that me learneth to love and suffer,
And wills that my trust and lust's negligence
Be reined by reason, shame, and reverence,
With his hardiness taketh displeasure.
Wherewithal, unto the heart's forest he fleeth,
Leaving his enterprise with pain and cry;
And there him hideth, and not appeareth.
What may I do when my master feareth
But in the field with him to live and die?
For good is the life ending faithfully.

To My Dear and Loving Husband

ANNE BRADSTREET

If ever two were one, then surely we.
If ever man were lov'd by wife, then thee.
If ever wife was happy in a man,
Compare with me, ye woman, if you can.
I prize thy love more than whole mines of gold,
Or all the riches that the east doth hold.
My love is such that rivers cannot quench,
Nor ought but love from thee give recompence.
Thy love is such I can no way repay;
The heavens reward thee manifold I pray.
Then while we live, in love let's so perséver,
That when we love no more, we may live ever.

THE DEFINITION OF LOVE

The Definition of Love

Andrew Marvell

My Love is of a birth as rare
As 'tis for object strange and high:
It was begotten by Despair
Upon Impossibility.

Magnanimous Despair alone
Could show me so divine a thing,
Where feeble Hope could ne'er have flown
But vainly flapped its tinsel wing.

And yet I quickly might arrive
Where my extended soul is fixt,
But Fate does iron wedges drive,
And always crowds itself betwixt.

For Fate with jealous eye does see
Two perfect Loves; nor lets them close:
Their union would her ruin be,
And her tyrannic power depose.

And therefore her decrees of steel
Us as the distant poles have placed,
(Though Love's whole world on us doth wheel)
Not by themselves to be embraced.

Unless the giddy heaven fall,
And earth some new convulsion tear;
And, us to join, the world should all
Be cramped into a planisphere.

As lines so Loves oblique may well
Themselves in every angle greet:
But ours so truly parallel,
Though infinite, can never meet.

Therefore the Love which us doth bind
But Fate so enviously debars,
Is the conjunction of the mind,
And opposition of the stars.

Those Who Love

SARA TEASDALE

Those who love the most,
Do not talk of their love,
Francesca, Guinevere,
Deirdre, Iseult, Heloïse,
In the fragrant gardens of heaven
Are silent, or speak if at all
Of fragile inconsequent things.

And a woman I used to know
Who loved one man from her youth,
Against the strength of the fates
Fighting in somber pride
Never spoke of this thing,
But hearing his name by chance,
A light would pass over her face.

A Modest Love

SIR EDWARD DYER

The lowest trees have tops, the ant her gall,
  The fly her spleen, the little sparks their heat;
The slender hairs cast shadows, though but small,
  And bees have stings, although they be not great;
Seas have their source, and so have shallow springs;
And love is love, in beggars as in kings.

Where rivers smoothest run, deep are the fords;
  The dial stirs, yet none perceives it move;
The firmest faith is in the fewest words;
  The turtles cannot sing, and yet they love:
True hearts have eyes and ears, no tongues to speak;
They hear and see, and sigh, and then they break.

Walsinghame

Sir Walter Raleigh

As you came from the holy land
  of Walsinghame
Met you not with my true love
  By the way as you came?

How shall I know your true love
  That have met many one
As I went to the holy land
  That have come, that have gone?

She is neither white nor brown
  But as the heavens fair
There is none hath a form so divine
  In the earth or the air.

Such an one did I meet, good Sir,
  Such an Angelic face,
Who like a queen, like a nymph, did appear
  By her gait, by her grace.

She hath left me here all alone,
  All alone as unknown,
Who sometimes did me lead with her self,
  And me loved as her own.

What's the cause that she leaves you alone
  And a new way doth take;
Who loved you once as her own
  And her joy did you make?

I have loved her all my youth,
  But now old, as you see,
Love likes not the falling fruit
  From the withered tree.

Know that love is a careless child
  And forgets promise past,
He is blind, he is deaf when he list
  And in faith never fast.

His desire is a dureless content
  And a trustless joy
He is won with a world of despair
  And is lost with a toy.

Of womenkind such indeed is the love
  Or the word Love abused
Under which many childish desires
  And conceits are excused.

But true Love is a durable fire
  In the mind ever burning;
Never sick, never old, never dead,
  From itself never turning.

A Lecture Upon the Shadow

John Donne

Stand still, and I will read to thee
A lecture, love, in love's philosophy.
These three hours that we have spent,
Walking here, two shadows went
Along with us, which we ourselves produc'd.
But, now the sun is just above our head,
We do those shadows tread,
And to brave clearness all things are reduc'd.
So whilst our infant loves did grow,
Disguises did, and shadows, flow
From us, and our cares; but now 'tis not so.
That love has not attain'd the high'st degree,
Which is still diligent lest others see.

Except our loves at this noon stay,
We shall new shadows make the other way.
As the first were made to blind
Others, these which come behind
Will work upon ourselves, and blind our eyes.
If our loves faint, and westwardly decline,
To me thou, falsely, thine,
And I to thee mine actions shall disguise.
The morning shadows wear away,
But these grow longer all the day;
But oh, love's day is short, if love decay.
Love is a growing, or full constant light,
And his first minute, after noon, is night.

From "Merlin and Vivien"

Alfred, Lord Tennyson

In Love, if Love be Love, if Love be ours,
Faith and unfaith can ne'er be equal powers:
Unfaith in aught is want of faith in all.

It is the little rift within the lute,
That by and by will make the music mute,
And ever widening slowly silence all.

The little rift within the lover's lute,
Or little pitted speck in garner'd fruit,
That rotting inward slowly moulders all.

It is not worth the keeping: let it go:
But shall it? answer, darling, answer, no.
And trust me not at all or all in all.

The Clod and the Pebble

William Blake

"Love seeketh not itself to please,
Nor for itself hath any care,
But for another gives its ease,
And builds a Heaven in Hell's despair."

So sung a little Clod of Clay
Trodden with the cattle's feet,
But a Pebble of the brook
Warbled out these metres meet:

"Love seeketh only self to please,
To bind another to its delight,
Joys in another's loss of ease,
And builds a Hell in Heaven's despite."

Love

Samuel Daniel

Love is a sickness full of woes,
　All remedies refusing;
A plant that with most cutting grows,
　Most barren with best using.
　　Why so?
More we enjoy it, more it dies;
If not enjoyed, it sighing cries,
　　Heigh ho!

Love is a torment of the mind,
　A tempest everlasting;
And Jove hath made it of a kind
　Not well, nor full, nor fasting.
　　Why so?
More we enjoy it, more it dies;
If not enjoyed, it sighing cries,
　　Heigh ho!

Pastoral Dialogue

ANNE KILLIGREW

Remember when you love, from that same hour
Your peace you put into your lover's power;
From that same hour from him you laws receive,
And as he shall ordain, you joy, or grieve,
Hope, fear, laugh, weep; Reason aloof does stand,
Disabled both to act, and to command.
Oh cruel fetters! rather wish to feel
On your soft limbs, the galling weight of steel;
Rather to bloody wounds oppose your breast.
No ill, by which the body can be pressed
You will so sensible a torment find
As shackles on your captived mind.
The mind from heaven its high descent did draw,
And brooks uneasily any other law
Than what from Reason dictated shall be.
Reason, a kind of innate deity,
Which only can adapt to ev'ry soul
A yoke so fit and light, that the control
All liberty excells; so sweet a sway,
The same 'tis to be happy, and obey;
Commands so wise, and with rewards so dressed,
That the according soul replies "I'm blessed."

Never Love Unless

Thomas Campion

Never love unless you can
Bear with all the faults of man:
Men sometimes will jealous be
Though but little cause they see;
And hang the head, as discontent,
And speak what straight they will repent.

Men that but one saint adore
Make a show of love to more.
Beauty must be scorned in none,
Though but truly served in one:
For what is courtship but disguise?
True hearts may have dissembling eyes.

Men, when their affairs require,
Must awhile themselves retire;
Sometimes hunt, and sometimes hawk,
And not ever sit and talk.
If these and such-like you can bear,
Then like, and love, and never fear!

Love

Elizabeth Barrett Browning

We cannot live, except thus mutually
We alternate, aware or unaware,
The reflex act of life: and when we bear
Our virtue onward most impulsively,
Most full of invocation, and to be
Most instantly compellant, certes, there
We live most life, whoever breathes most air
And counts his dying years by sun and sea.
But when a soul, by choice and conscience, doth
Throw out her full force on another soul,
The conscience and the concentration both
Make mere life, Love. For Life in perfect whole
And aim consummated, is Love in sooth,
As nature's magnet-heat rounds pole with pole.

Bond and Free

ROBERT FROST

Love has earth to which she clings
With hills and circling arms about—
Wall within wall to shut fear out.
But Thought has need of no such things,
For Thought has a pair of dauntless wings.

On snow and sand and turf, I see
Where Love has left a printed trace
With straining in the world's embrace.
And such is Love and glad to be.
But, Thought has shaken his ankles free.

Thought cleaves the interstellar gloom
And sits in Sirius' disc all night,
Till day makes him retrace his flight,
With smell of burning on every plume,
Back past the sun to an earthly room.

His gains in heaven are what they are.
Yet some say Love by being thrall
And simply staying possesses all
In several beauty that Thought fares far
To find fused in another star.

I Loved You First

Christina Rossetti

I loved you first: but afterwards your love
  Outsoaring mine, sang such a loftier song
As drowned the friendly cooings of my dove.
    Which owes the other most? my love was long,
    And yours one moment seemed to wax more strong;
I loved and guessed at you, you construed me
And loved me for what might or might not be—
    Nay, weights and measures do us both a wrong.
For verily love knows not "mine" or "thine";
    With separate "I" and "thou" free love has done,
      For one is both and both are one in love:
Rich love knows nought of "thine that is not mine";
      Both have the strength and both the length thereof,
      Both of us, of the love which makes us one.

Let Me Not to the Marriage of True Minds

William Shakespeare

Let me not to the marriage of true minds
Admit impediments, love is not love
Which alters when it alteration finds,
Or bends with the remover to remove.
O no! it is an ever-fixed mark,
That looks on tempests and is never shaken;
It is the star to every wand'ring bark,
Whose worth's unknown, although his height be taken.
Love's not Time's fool, though rosy lips and cheeks
Within his bending sickle's compass come,
Love alters not with his brief hours and weeks,
But bears it out even to the edge of doom:
   If this be error and upon me proved,
   I never writ, nor no man ever loved.

Give All to Love

Ralph Waldo Emerson

Give all to love;
Obey thy heart;
Friends, kindred, days,

Estate, good-fame,
Plans, credit and the Muse,
—Nothing refuse.

'Tis a brave master;
Let it have scope:
Follow it utterly,

Hope beyond hope:
High and more high
It dives into noon,

With wing unspent,
Untold intent;
But it is a god,

Knows its own path
And the outlets of the sky.
It was never for the mean;

It requireth courage stout.
Souls above doubt,
Valor unbending,

It will reward,—
They shall return
More than they were,

And ever ascending.
Leave all for love;
Yet, hear me, yet,

One word more thy heart behoved,
One pulse more of firm endeavor,
—Keep thee today,

Tomorrow, forever,
Free as an Arab
Of thy beloved.

Cling with life to the maid;
But when the surprise,
First vague shadow of surmise

Flits across her bosom young,
Of a joy apart from thee,
Free be she, fancy-free;
Nor thou detain her vesture's hem,

Nor the palest rose she flung
From her summer diadem.
Though thou loved her as thyself,

As a self of purer clay,
Though her parting dims the day,
Stealing grace from all alive;

Heartily know,
When half-gods go,
The gods arrive.

Of Love

ROBERT HERRICK

How Love came in, I do not know,
Whether by th' eye, or eare, or no:
Or whether with the soule it came
(At first) infused with the same:
Whether in part 'tis here or there,
Or, like the soule, whole every where:
This troubles me: but I as well
As any other, this can tell;
That when from hence she does depart,
The out-let then is from the heart.

INDEX

Author Index

Title Index

About the Authors

Aphra Behn (1640-89): British novelist and dramatist, the first Englishwoman known to earn her living by writing.

William Blake (1757-1827): English poet, engraver, painter, and mystic, radically original in his time and the earliest figure in English Romanticism.

Anne Bradstreet (1612?-72): English-born poet of the Massachusetts Bay Colony. Her *The Tenth Muse Lately Sprung Up in America* was the first volume of original verse to be written in America.

Emily Brontë (1818-48): British writer best known for her novel *Wuthering Heights*.

Elizabeth Barrett Browning (1806-61): English poet. *Sonnets from the Portuguese* (1850) is a sonnet sequence addressed to her husband, Robert Browning.

Robert Browning (1812-89): English poet, one of the greatest poets of the Victorian era.

Robert Burns (1759-96): Scottish poet, considered the greatest of his nationality.

George Gordon, Lord Byron (1788-1824): English poet, one of the major figures of the Romantic era.

Thomas Campion (1567-1620): English poet and musician. He set many of his poems to music.

Thomas Carew (1595?-1639?): English poet, the first and one of the best of the Cavalier poets.

William Cartwright (1611-43): English poet, scholar, and playwright.

George Chapman (1559?-1634): English poet and playwright, the first to translate Homer into English.

John Clare (1793-1864): English poet; he long supported himself as a farm laborer and eventually went mad.

Samuel Taylor Coleridge (1772-1834): English poet and essayist, the intellectual spokesman for the Romantic movement.

Samuel Daniel (1562?-1619): English poet and dramatist; his contemporaries called him "well-languaged Daniels" because of the purity of his diction.

Emily Dickinson (1830-86): American poet of striking originality. Only seven of her nearly two thousand poems were published during her lifetime.

John Donne (1572?-1631): English poet, the first and the greatest of the metaphysical poets of the 17th century.

Michael Drayton (1563-1631): English poet, the first to write English odes in the manner of the Roman poet Horace.

William Drummond (1585-1649): Scottish poet, the first of that nationality to write deliberately in English.

Paul Laurence Dunbar (1872-1906): African-American poet and novelist.

Sir Edward Dyer (1543-1607): English courtier and poet.

Elizabeth I (1533-1603): queen of England (1558-1603) and author.

Ralph Waldo Emerson (1803-82): American writer best known for his essays and lectures.

Robert Frost (1874-1963): American poet, generally considered one of the greatest poets of the 20th century.

Robert Herrick (1591-1674): English Cavalier poet known for his pastoral and love lyrics.

Leigh Hunt (1784-1859): English journalist, essayist, poet, and political radical.

Helen Hunt Jackson (1830-85): American poet and novelist, a friend of Emily Dickinson.

Ben Jonson (1573-1637): English dramatist and poet. "Song to Celia" is from his play *Volpone*.

John Keats (1795-1821): English poet, one of the principal figures of the Romantic era.

Anne Killigrew (1660-85): English poet and painter, the subject of one of John Dryden's odes.

Louise Labé (1524?-66): French poet. Her *Oeuvres* was published in 1555.

Sidney Lanier (1842-81): American poet, critic, and musician, a native of Georgia who fought in the Civil War.

Richard Lovelace (1618-58): English Cavalier poet, imprisoned twice during the English Civil War.

Amy Lowell (1874-1925): American poet, critic, and biographer, a member of the distinguished Lowell family of New England.

Christopher Marlowe (1564-93): English dramatist and poet, considered the greatest figure in Elizabethan drama before Shakespeare.

Andrew Marvell (1671-78): English metaphysical poet.

George Meredith (1828-1909): English novelist, poet, and critic. His *Modern Love* (1862) is a sequence of fifty poems based on his own unhappy marriage.

Coventry Patmore (1823-96): English poet, best known for *Angel in the House*, a poetic celebration of married life.

Edgar Allan Poe (1809-49): American poet, critic, and short-story writer. "Annabel Lee" is addressed to Virginia Clemm, whom Poe married when she was thirteen.

Sir Walter Raleigh (1552?-1618): English explorer, courtier, poet, and prose writer.

Lizette Woodworth Reese (1856-1935): American poet.

Christina Rossetti (1830-94): English poet. She often modeled for painters in the Pre-Raphaelite Brotherhood.

Dante Gabriel Rossetti (1828-82): English poet and painter, the brother of Christina Rossetti.

William Shakespeare (1564-1616): English dramatist and poet; most of the poems in this anthology are taken from his *Sonnets* (1609).

Mary Wollstonecraft Shelley (1797-1851): English novelist, best known for her Gothic novel *Frankenstein* (1818). She was the second wife of Percy Bysshe Shelley.

Percy Bysshe Shelley (1792-1822): English poet, a major figure of the Romantic movement.

Elizabeth Siddal (d. 1862): Wife and model for painter Dante Gabriel Rossetti, who buried her manuscript of poems with her when she died in 1862. It was exhumed in 1869 and published as *The House of Life*.

Sir Philip Sidney (1554-86): English poet, scholar, soldier, and courtier. His *Astrophel and Stella* (1591) created a vogue for the sonnet sequence in England.

Edmund Spenser (1552?-99): English poet, best known for his book-length epic *The Faerie Queen*. His *Amoretti* is a collection of sonnets.

Sir John Suckling (1609-42): English poet, courtier, and soldier, another of the Cavalier poets.

Henry Howard, Earl of Surrey (1517?-47): English poet and courtier attached to the court of Henry VIII.

Sara Teasdale (1884-1933): American poet; withdrawn in her later years, she eventually committed suicide.

Alfred, Lord Tennyson (1809-92): English poet, created Poet Laureate in 1850 by Queen Victoria. "Merlin and Vivien" is a chapter from his book-length poem *Idylls of the King*.

Thomas, Lord Vaux (1510-56): Early English Tudor poet, associated with Sir Thomas Wyatt and the Earl of Surrey.

Edmund Waller (1606–87): English poet, whose love lyrics were published in *Poems* (1645).

Ella Wheeler Wilcox (1850–1919): American poet and journalist.

George Wither (1588–1667): English poet and Puritan pamphleteer.

William Wordsworth (1770–1850): English poet, appointed Poet Laureate in 1843.

Sir Thomas Wyatt (1503–42): Tudor poet who introduced many Continental verse forms into English literature. Like the Earl of Surrey, he was a member of the court circle of Henry VIII.

AMERICAN LITERATURE

Little Women — Louisa May Alcott
The Last of the Mohicans — James Fenimore Cooper
The Red Badge of Courage and Maggie — Stephen Crane
Selected Poems — Emily Dickinson
Narrative of the Life and Other Writings — Frederick Douglass
The Scarlet Letter — Nathaniel Hawthorne
The Call of the Wild and *White Fang* – Jack London
Moby-Dick — Herman Melville
Major Tales and Poems — Edgar Allan Poe
The Jungle — Upton Sinclair
Uncle Tom's Cabin — Harriet Beecher Stowe
Walden and *Civil Disobedience* — Henry David Thoreau
Adventures of Huckleberry Finn — Mark Twain
The Complete Adventures of Tom Sawyer — Mark Twain
Ethan Frome and *Summer* — Edith Wharton
Leaves of Grass — Walt Whitman

WORLD LITERATURE

The Divine Comedy — Dante Alighieri
Tales from the 1001 Nights — Sir Richard Burton
Don Quixote — Miguel de Cervantes
Crime and Punishment — Fyodor Dostoevsky
The Count of Monte Cristo — Alexandre Dumas
The Three Musketeers — Alexandre Dumas
The Iliad — Homer
The Odyssey — Homer
The Hunchback of Notre-Dame — Victor Hugo
Les Misérables — Victor Hugo
The Phantom of the Opera — Gaston Leroux
The Prince — Niccolò Machiavelli

BRITISH LITERATURE

Emma — Jane Austen
Pride and Prejudice — Jane Austen
Sense and Sensibility — Jane Austen
Peter Pan — J. M. Barrie
Jane Eyre — Charlotte Brontë
Wuthering Heights — Emily Brontë
Alice in Wonderland — Lewis Carroll
Robinson Crusoe — Daniel Defoe
A Christmas Carol and Other Holiday Tales — Charles Dickens
Great Expectations — Charles Dickens
A Tale of Two Cities — Charles Dickens
A Passage to India — E. M. Forster
The Sonnets and Other Love Poems — William Shakespeare
Three Romantic Tragedies — William Shakespeare
Frankenstein — Mary Shelley
Dr. Jekyll and Mr. Hyde and Other Strange Tales — Robert Louis Stevenson
Treasure Island — Robert Louis Stevenson
Dracula — Bram Stoker
Gulliver's Travels — Jonathan Swift
The Time Machine and *The War of the Worlds* — H. G. Wells
The Picture of Dorian Gray — Oscar Wilde

ANTHOLOGIES

Four Centuries of Great Love Poems

The text of this book is set in 11 point Goudy Old Style, designed by American printer and typographer Frederic W. Goudy (1865–1947).

The archival-quality, natural paper is composed of recyclable products made from wood grown in sustainable forests; the manufacturing processes conform to the environmental regulations of the country of origin.

The finished volume demonstrates the convergence of Old-World craftsmanship and modern technology that exemplifies books manufactured by Edwards Brothers, Inc. Established in 1893, the family-owned business is a well-respected leader in book manufacturing, recognized the world over for quality and attention to detail.

In addition, Ann Arbor Media Group's editorial and design services provide full-service book publication to business partners.